Books by Ved Mehta

Face to Face
Walking the Indian Streets

WALKING
THE
INDIAN
STREETS

WALKING THE INDIAN STREETS

By

VED MEHTA

An Atlantic Monthly Press Book

Little, Brown and Company
BOSTON • TORONTO

Most of the material, in somewhat different form, ap-
peared originally in the *New Yorker*.

ATLANTIC–LITTLE, BROWN BOOKS
ARE PUBLISHED BY
LITTLE, BROWN AND COMPANY
IN ASSOCIATION WITH
THE ATLANTIC MONTHLY PRESS

*Published simultaneously in Canada
by Little, Brown & Company (Canada) Limited*

PRINTED IN THE UNITED STATES OF AMERICA

To
Christopher Hill
and
R. W. Southern

This book owes its life to two literary midwives: Joan Hartman and Harriet Yarrow. I am indebted to Joan Hartman for her friendship, suggestions, helpful and sometimes stubborn criticism, and to Harriet Yarrow for being a model amanuensis and for her patience and understanding in typing and retyping the manuscript.

CONTENTS

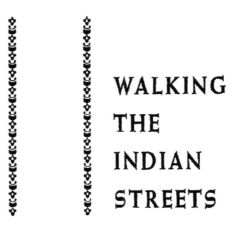

WALKING
THE
INDIAN
STREETS

I | HOME- COMING

A LETTER from an ancient and religious aunt who has ignored my existence for many years comes in the morning post.

"Dear Child," it reads, "You will be coming home after ten years. How you must have grown. I hope you are still my fifteen-year-old darling and love me as you did before. I think Ram came home after fourteen years' banishment, having fought and conquered evil in the jungles, and the people enjoyed and celebrated his return with candles and with bonfires. They say that when he returned the earth glowed like the sun. I hope you still remember and read the *Ramayana*, our great religious epic. Maybe you don't though. Boys get corrupted by the West."

My old aunt goes on, but I really have no time to read the letter properly. I am just in the middle of studying for Oxford finals, reading the notes on my index cards. I put the letter beside me and start thumbing through 4 x 6's. I go through hundreds of cards, reading of Alfred, of John and Henry VIII, of Elizabeth, Cromwell, and Gladstone. There isn't any time for my aunt, so I bury her among my index cards, along with other late Hanoverians.

I ought to explain that if I had received the same letter two years before, it would have been an occasion for self-analysis and self-mortification. It would have made me look in my mirror and I would not have enjoyed watching the image before me. I should have brooded over my own shortcomings.

But in these two years something has happened to me. The previous intensity of my feelings seems to have faded into the leisurely habits of Oxford. When I arrived at Oxford, I was crew-cut innocence abroad. I sprang out of bed at the healthy hour of seven, drank milk with breakfast, lunch, and dinner, and was in bed, reading and sleeping before midnight.

I submitted to the influences of Oxford when I started breaking up my afternoon work for a cup of tea at four. Then followed a cup of coffee after dinner. Sometimes I let myself be persuaded to coffee after lunch also. Then came sherry before dinner, first on week ends, then on weekdays. I enjoyed, now and again, taking some wine with dinner, brandy with coffee, and on special occasions, like a good party, I was prevailed upon to take punch with a gin base or even a Scotch.

I never drank very much because it made me feel tired and also because the pressure of work never let up. When I did take a coffee or tea break, or have a beer in Hall, I often became less serious and intense and more social and convivial. And this was splendid, because friendships and attachments came easily and I abandoned introspection for gossip and whimsy.

The English apparently know how to be casual and witty at the same time. For myself, I found at first the strain of making witty remarks sometimes too much, but by persevering I developed the ability to pick up the last remark and turn it in a funny and unexpected direction. Often the wit was the result of clever, clever me, and when I was being unusually clever, I controlled the wit as if I were working marionettes. Sometimes, stringing along with the wooden English figures, I performed feats I little expected, and while I never thought all this was really changing me in any radical way, in time I became adept at exploiting my fancies. I began feeling, somehow, there were two me's. The playful me did not make the serious me less dependable, just less vulnerable, and I came to see the quick wisdom of a satirist in my own foolishness. My moods could change rapidly. I raced through the seasons of a year in two or three weeks or two or three months. Sometimes I ran through them backwards.

So, you see, my aunt's letter in the middle of finals was extremely inconvenient. But when they were over, I began to look for it. In memory it seemed to be more Indian than anything I had received from home in some years, and although I hadn't read the *Ramayana* recently I began to think I should.

But before that — summer clothes. I go down to my tailors, distinguished tailors for young English gentlemen, and ask them to fit me out with some summer clothing. "Now, sir," the cutter says to me, "I understand you are going to the tropics. How would you like a Prince of Wales design? That is what we sold to the aide-de-camp of the last viceroy, and there has never been any complaint." But I want something simple. "Then, sir, I recommend some fawn-colored material. It is quite appropriate." I remind the cutter that I am really an Indian and, as far as possible, when in India expect to be taken for an Indian and not a dandified actor. We settle on an honest tropical wool.

The cutter and the tailor attend me in a side room. The tailor fixes me squint-eyed. I feel like an object about to be cunningly displayed. Sometime later, when I pick up the suit, I feel a bit embarrassed wearing it. The honest wool has been subtly altered.

The evening before my flight a Pakistani gentleman comes to bid me good-by. My artistic suit hangs in the clothes press — he wears his. I am interested in him as a guide to what I can expect at home for recently he, too, has returned. Like an American who sits next to you on a train, he easily unfolds his story.

After some years in an English university an English firm offers him a job. He refuses it for nationalistic reasons and joins the Pakistan Civil Service at one third the English salary. Some of his Anglophobe superiors hate him for being a gentleman and post him in a forsaken district of an unfamiliar province. Part of his duty consists of dispensing justice and he feels he is good at this because of his English education. The Pakistanis despise him for this education but paradoxically some years ago returned him to England for further training; like him, caught between East and West, they are torn in their loyalties.

He washes down tumblers of whiskey while I'm nursing one social drink. He went home to serve his country and returned to England an alcoholic.

"I've always loved my women and my whiskey," he explains, "but in my district there are no women.

7

I dispense licenses for the whiskey, so I give myself five bottles of Scotch a month, which costs twice my Civil Service pay. But my daddy pays with his black-market money, which I indulgently accept."

In preparing himself for service in Pakistan he tried, in his last year at Oxford, to give up drink. But he finds no support or encouragement in Pakistan — the time hangs heavy and the evenings are numb with inactivity.

"I still try to give it up," he insists, "but at six o'clock a thousand bells ring in my head, something happens to the pupils of my eyes, I feel tired and my head aches." Drinking for Muslims is like eating beef for Hindus, so he can't drink in public. "At six," he confesses, "I lock the doors, I pull down the shades and pour out a quarter of a bottle into a big mug. I turn on the Voice of America and start drinking my way out of Pakistan. When I begin to feel merry I dance a lonely dance to the Voice of America music. I despise myself, but I can't help it.

"I eat late," he continues, "at eleven, twelve o'clock. I nurse the mug as long as I can. You can't keep whiskey secret from your bearer. 'Sahib,' my bearer says to me one day, 'we expected people to be drunkards during the British raj, but we thought in our new Islamic republic things would be different.' I had to frighten him — he held my job and my reputation in his hands at that moment. The government won't keep you if they know you drink. I went over to the sideboard and picked up two empty whiskey bottles. 'If you say another word about this,' I screamed, 'I will crack your head open with these bottles.' Sobbing, the bearer fell at my feet, kissed my boots, and prayed to Mohammed. I have never done anything so horrible in my life. All my education — what was it for?"

Pain throbs in his whiskey-soaked eyes. I feel the terrible alienation imposed on him by his English clothes and his English vision. Drink befogs the issue but cannot dull the pain. He leaves me depressed and reflective.

Everyone must belong, yet those of us who were born in the twilight of the British raj were wounded for life. As children we were intimidated by well-spoken English and flattered by invitations to play at English houses because we were told these invitations were a mark of the highest success. We grew up thinking that white men were better than brown men, that a dark child in the family was less blessed than one with a fairer complexion. We grew up with a dream of going to England and catching a glimpse of Oxford and Cambridge spires. The setting of the British sun left us with an intellectual contempt for English values, but emotionally we were too far committed to withdraw. Our whole generation was sacrificed to a country in transition and we were condemned to live with a permanent hangover. My Pakistani friend was not alone in having no sense of belonging.

I barely catch the flight. We go up and up. The atmosphere is stifling, and the presence of the Anglo-Indian hostesses annoying. England drops away beneath the wings, and India, the India I knew years ago, explodes in my consciousness. Painful memories stand out: Uncertain freedom in 1947 and misgivings whether the country would be politically and economically viable. Partition in 1947 and Hindus and Sikhs murdered or, by the millions, dispatched to India; partition, 1947, and Muslims murdered or, by the millions, fleeing homeless to Pakistan. 1947, and more millions of Muslims choosing to remain in Gandhi's India. January 30th, 1948, India deprived of a great leader and a saint. Prime Minister Nehru, bent from the blow, pronounces, "The light has gone out of our lives."

Then there are years of estrangement — waiting in foreign places and asking questions about Gandhi's secular and casteless India, asking questions about changes — in constitution, in leadership, in economics. There are also personal memories — textbook history involved with family recollections.

Home-Coming

We, Hindus living in Pakistan, were forced to flee, leaving behind us all our property and faith in the ability of Hindu and Muslim ever to live side by side.

I must now get everything into focus. It is not easy to find a way back home after long absence. There are the subtle national changes. There is the aging and breaking up of the family — the death of my grandmother, the marriages of many. There is the alienation of education and vocabulary, of time and space.

Prague is called, then Rome, Beirut. In Damascus I get off the plane and order coffee. Flies fat as rats catch sight of me with their four thousand eyes. They sit on my nose, brush my eyelashes, caress my forehead. "Never mind the coffee," I say, and I rush back to the plane.

Vast stretches of the Indian Ocean move into view. It is hard to see from the plane. I can see, but barely, the hundreds of ships, their flags flying high, carrying silks, spices, and jewels to imperial England.

Cinema India, the India I have lived with in the years of exile, slides into focus. The voice is the narrator's, the English is the Queen's, and the accent is unmistakably upper-class.

Walking the Indian Streets

"India is a land of paradoxes, contradictions, extremes: on one hand, there are the Himalayan ranges — fifteen hundred miles across, thousands of feet high, almost as cold as the Antarctic; on the other, there is the Decca India — three months hot and nine months hotter still, flat as the desert. There is the Gangetic plain, fertile as any delta. There are heat waves and monsoons. The parching sun and four hundred inches of rain a year. Poverty of the people and the rich extravagances of the Maharajas (six hundred wasteful and dissipated principalities before India's independence). Clubs as leisurely as any in St. James's and slums as squalid as any in the East End. The Gandhi ascetic India and the begging, hungry India. The brown northerners of Aryan stock with straight hair, blue-brown eyes, thin lips, clear features — all the marks of successful invaders. And the Negroid southerners — fugitive Dravidians from the Gangetic plain with kinky hair, turned-up noses and thick lips. This is India.

"Here are its religions: Mohammedans, physical and militant, turn their eyes five times a day westward to Mecca. Fraternal like their Semitic brethren. They give unquestioning and complete obedience to the mullah and the mosque. They believe in God and have one sacred book; their heaven is rich with physical adornments — oases flowing with milk and honey; and Omár Kháyyám is their sensuous philosopher. They believe even more strongly than Catholics or Calvinists that all nonbelievers, whether shown the light or not, are damned heretics. These are the Mohammedans. This is India.

"Here are the Hindus: More gods than can sit on Olympus. No single book. An eclectic belief in universal salvation — the same for murderers and saints, monkeys and bears. Indisputable reverence for life in any form — life purified through cycles of reincarnation. And with this reverence for life, this belief in salvation for all, the caste system. These are the Hindus. This is India.

"This is the caste system whose origins lie in history and religion. The conquering Aryans made slaves of the Dravidians in the Gangetic plain. The Dravidians fled south and enslaved the Aborigines. Browned Aryans, black Dravidians, and blacker Aborigines — this is the source of caste and class. This invidious system becomes part and parcel of the Hindu cycle of reincarnation. A social issue becomes a burning religious question. This is the caste system. This is India.

"Her history encompasses saint and savage: Buddha, the high priest of nonviolence, and Asoka, the greatest and godliest of the world's emperors. Then Mahmud of Ghazni, hit-and-run conqueror and

Mohammedan auctioneer of Hindu women. Passive, peaceful India stands still in front of his assault, yields gradually to his Mohammedan successors. Most Indian Mohammedans are converts from Hinduism — converted rule the unconverted in the magnificent Mughal empire. Then decline of empire, India wracked with disunity, East India Company, Sepoy Mutiny of 1857, the sun of the British Empire. In the twentieth century, renaissance at last, led by Tagore and Gandhi. World wars flame the fire of liberation. This is India.

"New and old jostle each other. Astrology and astronomy. Ancient ruins; modern wonders. Uncovered archeological treasures and new air-conditioned trains. This is India."

Great stuff. This is cinema India. This is skin-deep and depthless India.

Delhi is announced and the nose of the plane bends down, dives, glides, and then comes to a dead halt.

More than a hundred relatives gather for the ceremony of my return. From a distance they seem indistinct and I have lost their faces in the years of separation. As I leave the plane and walk toward them, they pelt me with flowers. I stand there circled with garlands which, like snowdrifts, rise from

14

my feet to my eyebrows. I am imprisoned in the circle of flowers and relatives. Then I am swept away, and dozens of beggars following our progress through the flowers are rewarded with coins. The beggars disperse with cheerful faces and invoke the gods to bless our munificence. We are all bundled into old cars and, like a marriage procession, amble across the hot plains toward the city and home.

At home things are different. All the houses in the colony are newly built and their modest façades remind me that I am one of the refugees from Pakistan. Our new home is a feeble shadow of the old: small in size, without a compound, and with two rather than a dozen servants.

The rites of welcome continue at home. Sweetmeats, previously blessed, are served to all, and music is demanded. The music master sits in the center of the drawing room beside his harmonium and his boy disciple rubs his feet. I recall his face from Pakistani days and greet the Guru by touching his feet. He sweeps all the relatives aside, looks at me, and preens himself on his handiwork. "I taught him music when he was five. I was his first master!" he exclaims.

He makes me sit down on the floor beside him and then rapidly and nervously performs his songs. Distant relatives, one by one, straggle away, press-

ing remembrances and invitations upon me. Young
nieces and nephews are put to bed. While three
brothers-in-law and a new sister-in-law stand in
waiting, the original family, the refugees from Pakistan, weave around the master a garland of praise.

Now the master breaks into songs reminiscent
of happier days. Warming his voice to the past,
he sings long-forgotten melodies. There are battle
marches and coy wedding songs, women at the well
sing in the spring, a child lost from his mother calls,
farmers snip the corn with crisp tunes, a mother
mourns at the funeral of her child and prays to God
for his good reincarnation. We are carried back to
the old family ways. My sisters, now mothers, laugh
and cry like schoolgirls. We all remember the happy
days before division and freedom.

The night draws the curtain between the past
and the present, and the sisters depart to their several homes, leaving us reduced in number and happiness. The master muses: "Change is the way of
the world. It stands still only in music."

Schoolgirls grow up to be women, exchange
books for children. All must take separate ways if
they are not to grow into unhappiness together.
And that is natural.

The music master, the conjurer of the past, leaves
with his disciple, who carries the harmonium on his

head. He promises to return when he can. I go to bed on the veranda, for it is too hot to sleep inside. He will return, and so will my sisters with their husbands and their children, but his music is too frail to support the old happiness always.

II SITTING ON THE ISSUES

INDIA has an uncanny way of bringing out extremes in people, I suppose because we have been afflicted and enriched by centuries of migrations, moved like a pawn between this ruler and that. Our capacity for a single allegiance has been dulled. Instead we have developed an ability to be compassionate and cruel, sensitive and callous, deep and fickle. To untrained eyes we look colorful and picturesque, to critical eyes we appear shoddy imitations of our various masters. They miss our depth and complexity. We may have divided sensibilities, but we have also a relation between heart and head foreign to more civilized countries across the Indian Ocean.

The writer Han Suyin comments somewhere that Asians are like onions. They fatten, layer upon layer, over the centuries. Strip them, layer by layer, and there are still more layers to go. I agree with her; traveling through India I feel like an onion. There is the English me hankering after Oxford happiness. And there is the Indian me wishing to find a place in his own society. At first I'm frightened of exploring too deeply. England-returned Indians display me eagerly as an Oxford article, and for a while it is easy to drift and drink in their society. I easily accept their judgment that there is unconscious resentment against returning natives educated abroad and that a host of prejudices will prevent Anglicized Indians from becoming natives. It is easier to believe than to probe with uncertain touch.

But the Indian patriot nags at the English expatriate. I try to find my way back to the heart of India by walking and talking and listening to friends, politicians, and men in the crowd. I have never before felt the press of problems and people as here. I can't walk the streets. They are crowded with venders, hawkers, servants shopping for their masters, little boys getting their education from gaunt men who seem to know everything about life and who laugh cunningly as they pass on the wisdom of the streets.

The wisdom of my disappointed expatriate friends is more lucidly phrased; the country is diseased and overpeopled and they blame history and politicians. They say, "At the beginning of the century we had a little over one half the present population, just enough for the irrigated land. We had good masters in the English. They did not understand us but they believed in justice, law and order, and the Indians did not know English well enough to approach them with graft. They weren't burdened with poor relations in India — most of them came to rule singly. But look around you now. Everywhere there is corruption and nepotism. Gandhi is dead and with him our enthusiasm for freedom." Some expatriates, trying to outdo the patriots, add, "Communism alone can restore our moral confidence." They are not alone in their complaint. Each morning the English-language papers proclaim to their educated readers in banner headlines about political storms everywhere. There is Kerala and Communism, General Thimmaya versus Krishna Menon, China and yellow imperialism. The text develops the themes "Evils of Party Government," "Incurable Wrongs," and "Democracy on the Way Out."

An All India Radio broadcast claims that caste relationships remain unchanged and Gandhi's great struggle on behalf of the untouchables, whom he called Harijans (Children of God), has been lost and forgotten. The Children of God are still not permitted into the Brahmin temples. Pundits and Cassandras forecast a civil war between northern and southern India, between the so-called Aryan and Dravidian races. The fanatics in Punjab, like Tara Singh, herald a secession movement for the Sikhs, and other fanatics in India urge a holocaust of Muslims to make the motherland safe for the Hindu majority. Someone compares Nehru in India to Noah in his ark, Noah, who by his partitions kept the lions from the lambs; someone else says, "Outcome is uncertain." Yet another confidently predicts, "All lights will truly go out with Nehru's death," and there is an even more fatuous prediction in a two-year-old Punjabi newssheet which I find covering a cupboard shelf, that beginning with 1957, the hundredth anniversary of the Indian mutiny, there will be twelve years of total darkness in India during which all the Muslims will be massacred and their remains used to fertilize bumper crops. For myself, I disregard the prophecies but am disturbed by the presence of the prophets.

In my first days in Delhi I meet a number of my family's friends, some of whom are Muslims. I am glad to see that our family, though they are victims of Muslim persecution, have made Muslim friends. These Muslims think of India as home because they have known no other, are Indians before Muslims. But they are concerned lest the possibility of Gandhi's secular India, after Nehru, will pass into the hands of fanatics and religious purists. Pakistan they regard as the unfortunate legacy of the British raj, which ultimately parceled out the country on the theory that Hindus and Muslims would need separate nations. The theory was naïve because Muslims were dispersed throughout India and almost half of them did not wish to be uprooted in order to create a separate nation. Kashmir, predominantly Muslim, first joined India and now would join Pakistan — the tidy British formula produced snarled loyalties and an issue to intensify the hatred between the two nations. War between Pakistan and India over Kashmir would destroy the Indian Muslims, who would not know whether to put national above religious loyalties. Even the threat of war jeopardizes the secular Indian state by keeping open the Hindu-Muslim question.

I catch one of these family friends and listen to his real fears, which are not discussed in the national newspapers. He works for an English firm with offices in India and Pakistan. Part of his family has emigrated to Pakistan already, but so far he remains in India. His speech is fluent, his analysis keen. "The free India has treated us better than we have any right to expect, but perhaps the government has been too conciliatory and too judicious. While archaic Hindu laws on marriage and caste, for example, have been brought up to date, Muslim laws have been left untouched. Like the British, our government has been too sensitive about religious practices. I am certain that if Hindus will not force Muslims to reform, they will never reform themselves, and before the Muslims know it they will be a backward minority, and, just as Hindus blame their social backwardness and archaic laws on the British, so the Muslims will blame theirs on the Hindus. The faults may be Muslim, but I doubt that the cursed generations of the future will remember this. I am afraid of a Hindu raj." My Muslim friend explains to me that the newspapers can't discuss these questions openly. Eight million refugees who have fled Pakistan since partition carry with them inflammable memories.

I find the newspapers and magazines too grim, and search them for theater criticism and reviews of musical events, poetry and fiction, but there is little of that because, as I keep reminding myself, culture needs affluence and leisure and India is a poor country.

Gossip is as abundant as light and travels at the speed of light. "An important politician attends all his official meetings in his pajamas. He needs frequent injections because of some internal trouble and it is a common sight for the civil service grandees to see him undo his pajama cord and take hip injections while he harangues them about lapses in duty among the civil servants or about the disloyalty of corrupt sanitary inspectors." "He calls all the grandees, contemptuously, 'clerks.'" "His relatives are known hooligans. They gamble, they abduct women, they live in several sins."

And so the political gossip goes, until some state capitals seem political circuses and hotbeds of corruption.

I have been doing some free-lance writing for the *Statesman,* last of the English-owned papers in India. England seems to be well covered, so I write about America. My writing is a passport to politicians who would be inaccessible otherwise. For my edification I sit and drink coffee and talk to Evan Charlton, the Delhi publisher of the *Statesman.* As an expatriate, I find it easier to begin my political education with an Englishman who has worked on newspapers both in British and Free India. To the peons he speaks a bizarre Hindi which I associate with the English in India. He is devoted to Nehru's India and the Commonwealth. He expands on India's progress. Aeroplanes are a great thing in India. Our country is linked and united as never before. A letter can be sent to Calcutta today and

get there tomorrow, and a parliamentary committee can fly across to Madras in a few hours. The big
dams will make this country more fertile than ever
before, and the people will be fed. The grass-roots
work of building the nation is being done everywhere, in the villages, in various kinds of schools
for boys and girls, in women's colleges. Charlton
has the feeling that India is producing better women
than men. The reason may be that men came in
more direct contact with the British raj than did the
women. While the men may have been Anglicized
and crippled, the women remained Indian; their
seduction by the British stopped with lipstick and
fingernail polish. A great strength of Gandhi's non-
violent movement was the equality of men and
women within it. In the West women were liberated by industrial society, in India by passive disobedience.

I continue my political education with a visit to
the President of India, a shy, simple leader, born and
educated in India and instinctively Gandhian in his
ways. I sit beside Rajinder Prasad in the stately
palace built for the British viceroys and the saintly
President seems out of place in its imperial splendor.
I ask him how he entered political life and what
divides British from Free India.

He reminisces. He was a successful lawyer in

Behar when Mahatma Gandhi arrived in the province to settle a labor dispute on the rice plantations. Gandhi was on the side of the workers, Prasad was on the side of the owners, and then one day they came together from their two different sides and Gandhi talked to him for ten or fifteen minutes and he was a different man. "Before meeting Gandhiji, my aims, like those of all parents, were a good standard of living and the best of education for my children, and I was in a position to achieve them, but after meeting him, these things that were important earlier were important no more. My wife and children were no longer the first things in my life."

Had this meeting made him indifferent to personal happiness? "You don't understand. After that meeting I relinquished everything to follow the movement, which gave me more personal happiness than anything before. Once I took up the cause there was no time left to think about my children and their education." His giving himself to politics was a "testament to Gandhiji's miraculous power. Gandhiji had a way of making leaders out of clay. Everyone who came in contact with him became a leader. But now he is gone."

Outside the palace of the past viceroys, I stop and chat with the President's aide-de-camp, who talks of the President's coming tour. Prasad is the Lincoln of India. Above all he wishes to preserve the Union. Since our leaders realize that our country is torn by its Hindu, Mughal and British images, the President always makes a point of spending Independence Day in the South while the Prime Minister celebrates it for the North at Red Fort.

The Red Fort is the ancient seat of the Mughals, and, with the Taj Mahal, it stands as a monument to the glories of the Muslim empire. Today its image must be accommodated in the new India. So it is that the Prime Minister on Independence Day climbs the ramparts of the Red Fort and, from this place of authority, talks to the people about the Union. The leaders of Free India live in the borrowed houses of Muslim and English rulers, and unless they learn to live in them comfortably India will disintegrate.

Next I find myself sitting across from a different kind of leader, one not schooled directly under Gandhi. He has his bare feet on the desk, a loincloth around his waist, and a cup of tea in his hand. The thin, hairy legs seem inappropriate in the air-conditioned atmosphere of Whitehall. The leader remarks that it is hard for poor Indians to fill the large offices of the English. But we cannot wish away the British India.

But I came to hear his views on the Hindu-Muslim dispute. Nothing is more important to me than a secular India. I am afraid that the religious harmony of Nehru's India may be destroyed by Kashmir. I ask whether there was ever a time when India could have exchanged Kashmir for a piece of Pakistani territory. By settling the dispute over Kashmir we would have made safe forever the lives of forty million Muslims now living in India and perhaps done something to heal the breach between Hindus and Muslims which robbed us of a united India and even of Gandhi himself.

"No, no," he snaps, "we can never compromise on Kashmir. Where do you start drawing the line? By feeding Pakistani appetites you whet them, and before you know it they will demand the Red Fort. This is not the way to run a country. We are in the middle of a power struggle with Pakistan. We must be firm."

But doesn't our Kashmir policy contain the threat of war? Many privately admit that if a plebiscite were held, Kashmir would go to Pakistan. We have already paid much more than Kashmir is worth to us. It doesn't seem sensible to me to apportion a large part of our small national budget for the defense of Kashmir. He replies, "If Kashmir were divided or surrendered to Pakistan today, it would mean refugees and riots once again, and the lives of those

forty million Muslims living in India would be anything but safe." I insist that the Kashmir issue, un-
resolved, will always hold this threat and that, in
preferring a status quo to a permanent settlement,
we are postponing the refugees and riots he dreads.
My own dread is that of my Muslim friend, and I
can see how at some time these forty million may
choose religious loyalty and so fulfill the prediction
of Hindu nationalists and fanatics by serving as a
Pakistani fifth column. He refuses to take my remarks seriously. "You have to put on more fat before you can hold weighty opinions like these," he
says. "Don't mistake me," he adds gently, "I'm not
anti-Muslim. If anything I am too pro-Muslim."

I stop him there and ask if this isn't the very thing
of which the Muslims complain. No one likes to be
treated with patronizing indulgence.

"You can't have it both ways. You can't claim a
privileged position and at the same time blame the
government for giving you the privileges. There are
many difficulties. All we can do is let sleeping dogs
lie — sit on the issues." But are Indian Muslims
really asking for a privileged position or are we being indulgent because we are afraid of them? How
can the secular state survive when we have separate
laws for different religious groups and when we
legislate that Hindus must be monogamous and

Muslims need not be? The Sikhs and untouchables ask for privileges equal to those of the Muslims. The Muslims are uneasy because of their privileges. And the leaders sit on the issues.

"What else is there to do? This is our heritage from the past." India is a country of many races, languages, and religions. Placate one religious minority or language group, all others make demands. There are so many empty stomachs here that any cause can get a following. There is only one historical parallel to our situation, the Austro-Hungarian empire which, like India, enclosed many minorities. It collapsed, leaving behind it splinter states from which rose ruthless dictators. The fanatics in our country who want an autonomous Dravidian state or those who want a separate Sikh state or some of those who would like the country to be partitioned according to language do not realize these dangers. The states would simply fall as prizes to dictators who will fight among themselves because their countries will not be economically viable. But how can you read history books to fanatics? India is one nation almost completely because of the Prime Minister. If the Prime Minister lives for some time and if there is no war between Pakistan and India we may still be able, by enlightened policy, to develop national loyalties.

Sitting on the Issues

"But," he admonishes, "you go along and have some words with our military people, wander through the bureaucracy and see our problems. We've only touched on some of them."

His aide-de-camp rings up a military chief and a few hours later I am conversing with the military people. I find myself in a building with secret chambers and shut doors, and while waiting for the chief I chat with his aide-de-camp (India has as many aide-de-camps as Americans have secretaries and, like the secretaries, the aide-de-camps really run the country). I ask the aide-de-camp what the cloak and dagger atmosphere indicates. "We have here a system of intercepting messages and breaking codes. There are strange inefficiencies in Pakistan. Just the other day there was a broadcast from Karachi to their formations in Kashmir directing them to change their position. The Pakistani signal operator shouted the coded message repeatedly but the reception was bad and the man at the receiving end didn't seem to understand very much. Finally, the signal operator blurted out, 'You mother sleeping sister sleeping! Can't you understand? I'm telling you to move the formations from —— to ——.' This is how we break the code. These Pakistani Muslims really lack control. They'll never learn and we'll always be one ahead of them."

Walking the Indian Streets

"You know," I say sententiously, "today Europe would be Muslim if it weren't for Charles Martel in 732."

"What did you say?" he says quizzically.

"You know, today Europe would be Muslim if it weren't for Charles Martel in 732."

"What does that have to do with Kashmir?"

By that time a shut door opens and I am led in to the chief. He sits down on a big sofa and talks about the dangers of military dictatorships. Pakistan, he tells me, is a military dictatorship, but India is different because the national army is devoted to Nehru's government. But danger is always there — the officers, at present devoid of political ambition, may acquire it. Am I aware there is some conflict between the political and military high command at this moment? In the army promotion by merit is everything. When a private joins the army he knows the exact proportion between ranks — so many privates to so many corporals, so many corporals to so many sergeants, and on up the ladder — and he calculates his chances of higher pay and rank accordingly. If a politician takes it into his head to promote this favorite or that, even if only one or two, the army as an organization is shattered. The faith of the private in his future is shattered. This is probably the story behind General Thimmaya's protest resignation. If the defense minister, Krishna Menon, had been playing political favorites, General Thimmaya had a good reason for his resignation. He was forced to retract his resignation because a democracy like ours cannot afford a truculent army, however just its grievances. Both the military and the politicians seem confused about what the relation between them is to be and whether the military can be left as an autonomous power with the potential of upsetting the government.

The main thing to remember is that India is surrounded by military dictatorships. Ceylon, Indonesia, and Pakistan all have been taken over by dictators. China presses from the north, Pakistan from east and west, and we are left to defend ourselves with weapons purchased abroad. The chief challenges me: "Has any nation ever successfully fought a war with bought weapons? The real defenses of a country are its industrial potential. Our industrial power is slight and we are faced with the two biggest enemies in the world. A war with Pakistan could enlist the resources and sympathies of the whole Islamic world. A war with China those of the Communist world. What would we have to draw upon? Obsolete weapons *Made in England*."

"What do you plan to do about it?" I ask.

"Nothing." Just sit on the issues. That's all you

can do in India — sit on the issues, sit on the defenses. Put on a front — feel big, act big and think big.

I leave the grave chief sitting on his sofa and go to the planning commission to find out how the economic theoreticians are going to reshape the country. I glean statistics and pore over pamphlets and plans. I learn that India of 1947 and Russia of 1917 bear no comparison. India has more than two times the population of Russia and one sixth the land to support it. Our country is excellent for growing grain and fruit. It has coal and iron and manganese and mica for large industries. But the population is rising too fast, seven million people more a year, and the problems of providing housing, food and education for these seven million are stupendous.

The Deputy Chairman of the Commission, Mr. V. T. Krishnamachari, explains that when figures get into millions they stop meaning anything. He tries to make me visualize half a million children born every month and his duty to provide a place in society for them. As for birth control, the present methods are too messy, too expensive. India must also sit on the population issue. He is angered when Western reporters call his five-year plans too ambitious. "Our present per capita income," he says, "is sixty dollars a year, and by 1975 we hope to have it up to a hundred and twenty dollars a year. Is this ambition?"

Krishnamachari thinks that the Western reporters have been far too enthusiastic about China's progress. He works continuously with facts and statistics and knows how they can be manipulated to give any conclusion. Until 1958 Chinese economists were working on false economic principles — "The more people, the better the country." Since then the economists have reversed themselves, but their false principles must have cost the Chinese something. Everyone knows that dictatorial methods are speedy and the Chinese have proved this by their campaign against "enemy fly" and "enemy sparrow." But a complete transformation of the economy from agrarian to industrial or from poor to rich takes time in a dictatorship or a democracy.

India's race with China is very important and the outcome will be touch-and-go. The victory of China is by no means a foregone conclusion, as some of the jittery reporters in the West make believe. In his learned way the Deputy Chairman sneers at Western reporters for their jargon — "P Bomb" for rising population. Such jargon simply makes people jittery. "We are not children that we have to re-

member things with alphabets." A for Apple con-
cludes the interview.

Formal interviews end in the face of a present
crisis in the state of Kerala. Kerala is in many ways
unique among the states of India. The only elected
Communist government. A high level of literacy —
almost sixty per cent of its people read and write,
while in the rest of the country twenty to twenty-
five per cent is the average. The only state predominantly Christian — instead of Hindu and Muslim,
a strong Catholic hierarchy. The Communists were
elected by an uneasy alliance with the church, then
turned on their allies and tried to make convent
education Marxist. Communists and Catholics run
foul of each other, violence erupts in the streets,
prisons overflow with Christians, and the central
government finally steps in to depose the state government.

I go to the lower house of Parliament, the House
of the People, to hear the debate on Kerala. Communist members shout excitedly. Democracy is
dead in India. All elections are a farce if govern-
ments can be deposed willy-nilly.

Prime Minister Nehru stands, and for endless
hours, unruffled by interruptions and jeers, he de-
fends the action of the central government. Some-

times people break out in laughter and sometimes
their faces are red with rage. Sometimes the air con-
ditioners go off. Sometimes, as in the bazaars, people shout at each other. The habit of shouting seems
Indian, not Anglo-Saxon, and I feel as if I were out
on the Indian streets instead of in the House of the
People.

The Prime Minister argues his case like a lawyer
and patiently outlines the disturbances in Kerala,
the misuse of power by the Communist government,
the debates of his cabinet, his conferences with the
Communist leaders, and his prolonged and futile
attempts to reach a solution without the interven-
tion of the central government. He speaks from
notes and seems to address the nation as well as the
parliament. His decision is not that of a dictator but
that of a responsible governor. The methods of the
Communists threaten democracy. I leave the debate
with a lively sense of democracy in practice in India. India cannot sit when democracy is threatened.

Mr. Jayaprakash Narayan comes to Delhi and the
journalists arrange a tea for him. When I left India,
after independence, he was the leader of the younger
generation, and theorist of the Socialist Party, and
an intellectual rival of the Prime Minister listened to
respectfully at home and abroad. The Prime Minis-

ter himself courted him for a time. His followers, who saw him as the probable successor to Nehru, were disappointed when he left politics to follow Vinoba Bahve, a new Gandhi, who walks from village to village collecting gifts of land from the landowners for redistribution to the landless. I remember Narayan as the politician rather than the saint.

The journalists of the leading newspapers — *Statesman, Times of India, Hindustan Times* and *Indian Express* — pick Narayan's brain. They sip their tea and prepare their editorials. Narayan commends the action of the central government in Kerala. Kerala is a laboratory experiment of Communist strategy. They will use constitutional means to grasp power but, once in power, they will abuse it. What the Communists did in Kerala is a good lesson for the masses. We have reason to be pleased. Frank Moraes, editor of the *Indian Express* and father of my Oxford friend Dom, explains to me that Narayan's remarks on Kerala are significant because of his political disinterestedness and his sainthood in the eyes of the people.

From Kerala the journalists press on to the threat of China. They recall that Narayan was one of the first to respond with feeling to the plight of the Dalai Lama. When the god of the Tibetan Buddhists fled his country and asked for a home in India for himself and his party, the government seemed embarrassed. What was to happen to the friendship of India and China, to amicable relations between the two countries?

(Moraes explains to me that the Prime Minister has not always been deluded by the tinsel promises of the peace-loving Chinese. Ten years ago Moraes was asked to go on a cultural mission to China. The Prime Minister took the delegates aside to say that China threatened not only the borders of India but the spine of Asia. If the Prime Minister has been inactive, he has either miscalculated the time when the Chinese could safely act on their hidden intentions or has felt helpless and tries, so far as possible, to prolong India's neutrality in order to transform the country. He may also have been deluded by some of his advisers into a wrong evaluation of the Chinese threat.)

Narayan admits to uncertainty about the Dalai Lama and China. He wonders what Nehru would have done if he had been an exile during the Indian Nationalist struggle and had been greeted with the chill reception accorded the Dalai Lama. While Narayan is distressed by the Prime Minister's prudent calculation, he realizes that the Chinese threat is paralyzing and that whatever the differences between himself and Mr. Nehru, India has little choice but to sit and wait.

India and China should go to a conference table.

India and China should try to reach new border agreements. India should be prepared to establish a Himalayan federation if that is the choice of the Himalayan peoples. "We cannot apply double standards in our foreign policy" he says. "We cannot protest on behalf of ruled colonies if we appear to create our own Himalayan protectorates in Nepal, Sikkim, and Bhutan."

We must sit and wait, but I find Narayan's posture uncomfortable. For a decade India has been self-appointed moral tutor to the world. She kept alive the cause of China, she lashed out on Suez, but she held her tongue on Hungary till it was too late. She harangued the world on idealism and diplomacy based on *realpolitik*. And all this time she had a skeleton in her cupboard. She was taking one stand about China in public but harboring, privately, quite a different view of her. If we must sit and wait, we can be more comfortably propped up by admitting our loyalties to the West. However great in size, we are helpless alone.

Narayan appears more and more uncomfortable as the discussion turns on politics and power. He moves to the saintlier grounds of the Bhoodan movement and delivers a sermon. Technology is as much a matter of the spirit as of invention. Technology must be humanized and the land-gift movement is the road to humanized technology. Gandhi had his face set against making India an industrial society. In his view the way to a new India was through village-home industry and village democracy, through a sense of pride in work, a sense of belonging to a community of work. Bhoodan is Gandhi's spirit in action — the lectures, the hymns, the marches, the meetings, the quiet haranguings to the collected landowners and the voluntary gifts of millions and millions of acres.

Narayan warms to his theme. Vinoba Bhave is working in Gandhi's tradition, a tradition of spiritual socialism which is to be the great gift of India to political thought. Bhoodan is not Utopian, it is a revolution at the grass roots, and Indian rather than Western in origin. "You can see the power of our new socialism," he says with soft pride, "when you talk to the landowners about the landless peasants, and appeal to the good in them."

Narayan admits that land proffered may be barren, may be in strips and therefore impractical for cultivation, but he argues that the movement is important in its tangible as well as in its spiritual power. I come away feeling the loss of Narayan the politician to Narayan the saint, but with the conviction that, in India, there may be more progress through spiritual appeal than through political legislation. In Narayan's own words, "Land reform is as much a matter of conscience as a matter of legislation, and conscience can only be aroused by appealing to the good in us." This is Gandhi's India, the India of the Ganges, the India of the ages, and Narayan is a real son of his country.

I walk out from the tea writing my own editorial, "Past and Present," but I don't think it is publishable in many Indian papers.

There are not enough Narayans in India, I write. Older men, including the President, write day in and day out of the degeneration of the Indian character since independence, of the growth of crime, poverty and hunger. They deplore the deterioration of politics in Free India, not so much in the center as in the fourteen states established by the Federal Constitution.

In these states, political offices are sometimes gained through greasing peasant palms. The politicians, when elected, use their offices to build an empire for their family and friends. Not many can afford disinterested action; they must instead cushion themselves against their return to the poverty of private life. An entire class of political entrepreneurs is emerging. In a country with little economic security, with high unemployment for men and hardly any employment for women, family is often put above national interest. Can liberal democracy survive in such a country? This is my question and this is my lament.

The list of India's difficulties is endless. If one is not a saint, one must grow callous to the life around and wander through India tongueless, with eyes shut, ears punctured. One must follow the example of the three wise monkeys — speak not, see not, hear not. Problems are too many and solutions too few. But man is not a monkey. With his reason and sensibilities, he must speak out or burst from the strain of keeping silence.

There is a terrible lack of urgency in India. Most of the books I have read about India miss the mark. Either they are too optimistic or too pessimistic about her future, and I think optimism is the more dangerous. If everyone keeps on talking about India with sympathetic optimism, we may be deluded long enough to permit democracy to slip away from us. We may soft-pedal ourselves into disaster.

If the Indian democracy is to survive, we must separate history from prejudice. We can never wish away the British raj. We can, but we should not, load on a British scapegoat our divisions and shortcomings. Our history is both British and Indian. We must commend the British for teaching us their language. Instead of ruling us as the Dutch did the Indonesians — Dutch officers did not even share language with their clerks — our rulers introduced us to the literature of revolt. It was a rare thing for an Indian educated under English masters not to be exposed, at one time or another, to John Stuart Mill's "Essay on Liberty." We acquired as political saints Milton, Mill and Shaw, and while the object of the English in educating us may have been nothing more than to staff the civil service with clerks, by their decision to teach these clerks English they extended to us a privilege whose consequences they could not completely foresee. Now, free from the British raj, we must at least thank them for this.

With these gains recognized we can more justly assess our losses. A subcontinent was ruled by a few thousand Englishmen and our history reduced to a subtopic in the chronicle of British imperialism. The English robbed us of a sense of history. We looked to our past in a spirit of ancestor worship and became indifferent to our present. In this heap of broken history we lost our identity.

In 1947, with independence, the present became our own. But some continue to prefer fancy to history. It is fanciful to think the British raj could have been prolonged to our advantage. A country cannot be made ready for freedom by her rulers; she must go it alone. It is fanciful to think that our freedom could have been won through violent revolution. Hungary showed that where a state commands modern means of destruction, violent revolution must fail. Revolution as a concept is outdated. Even if violent revolution were possible, it is even more fanciful to think that struggle would have kept India united. Though the British fostered division, they did not create it. Present movements to repartition the country on religious and linguistic lines demonstrate the disunity cleaving India. No, fancy is pleasant but history remains. History is India — independent, struggling, and disunited.

Present-day India must be a compromise. Peaceful revolution left us with British formulas. We avoided a violent break with the past and so were deprived of the Utopian energy of other revolutions. But we had a choice, to improve boldly on the old formulas or to apply them slavishly to problems too large for them. In drafting a constitution we audaciously revised them to our needs: a federal state within the commonwealth. But in clinging to a civil service more British than Indian, for example, we propped up our new country with dead history.

In compromise India, the old Indian civil service goes on. Its prestige and power are almost unrivaled in the free world. Its system is British born — admission by competition, promotion by tact and seniority — and its life reflects the feeble ideal of a public school in Victorian England. First the best minds are bought for the civil service, then they are reduced to a uniform talent. A public school boy must be good not only at cricket and classics but at strict obedience. A first secretary, if so ordered, should be able to clean the secretariat better than the charwomen. Only through unquestioning obedience can command be learned. The civil service runs like a military organization. Orders issued at any level must be obeyed by those below. Deference must be adjusted to the chain of command and everyone must know his station. The wife of a second secretary should cultivate the wife of number one and be condescending towards the wife of number three.

Empty conventions provide the pomp indispensable to the system. Carbon copies and files almost outnumber people — only the carbons are considered irreplaceable. Conventions, rules, precedents can never be waived. One exception will establish a rule and bind the Civil Service forever.

The English perpetuated this rigid system for their clerks, not themselves. But these Indian clerks, now officers, carry on the repressive tradition of Victorian England. They fear to speak their minds lest they jeopardize their promotion. No wonder many officers enjoy more their posts in the districts than promotion in the secretariat; at least in the districts they are in touch with people and problems.

Sitting on the Issues

Dispensing justice in individual cases, gathering statistics about a flood or a famine, delving into local records and working with them like historians, advising on the collection of taxes — all these are much more invigorating than sitting in Delhi. Decorum and the right degree of deference for officers, a rigid concept of rulers and ruled, remain the tenets of our new Administrative Service, while the civil services of other nations are abandoning them.

There are great and conspicuous exceptions to the civil service establishment. N. Raghavan Pillai, Secretary General, is one of them, but these exceptions are few and far between.

Unlike their English predecessors, many of the officers lack confidence and are afraid to make authoritative decisions without referring to their superiors. Responsibilities pass from hand to hand until someone has the courage to forget them. Often the Prime Minister is forced to be his own civil service. Little squabbles, a personal problem of this officer and that — all are appealed to him. For all its boasted efficiency, the civil service sits on the issues.

This service needs decentralized command, less concern with decorum, and more flexibility. It should be prepared to use unusual and creative talent. For many years it will remain the career of ambitious young men and women in India because in an economically insecure country government employment offers the only security. If we shrink from experiment and refuse to depart from old conventions, we may find ourselves reduced to carbon copies of the British raj.

The civil service, like so many things in India, is a hold-over from the tarnished glories of the British raj. We find it hard to live with, harder to live without. Our choice, I write, is to live with fake standards or with no standards at all, which is almost to say that the choice does not exist.

The absence of choice is the Indian blind alley of analysis, of intelligence. I come up against a granite wall of problems, but this does not prevent the serious me from having opinions or ideas. I disagree with the weak policy of Nehru's government toward China. I wish that in our diplomacy we were less philosophic and more realistic, that if we really were aware of the Chinese threat earlier, we had abandoned our isolationist policy, at least in part, and sought assistance from the Western powers. I regret fighting for a Pyrrhic victory in Kashmir. I differ with the government's soft-pedaling of the religious issue, which seems to gloss over the real problem of the Muslim minority and simply postpones the threat to the secular state. Indeed, I object to the too conciliatory policy towards minorities, whether religious or linguistic. I abhor the attachment of second-class politicians to the Prime Minister's person and his to his friends, friends who sometimes abuse his trust with impunity (this tolerance, while a very commendable personal trait, cannot be thought politically astute). I am impatient with his government for its small progress towards breaking down the caste barriers; with its failure to inject more creativity into the civil service. I even take exception to the Federal Constitution, which created as many legislatures and premiers as states, instead of a sensibly unified government for the nation. And, however justifiable the reasons, I am saddened by the dearth of a younger generation of leaders. But I can see why we must sit on some of these issues.

Because conditions cannot be changed and most problems remain insoluble, it is difficult to have national or personal identity, difficult to distinguish between correct feelings and wrong feelings. The Gandhian way is attractive but thorny. Sainthood is not easy, and asceticism is a rejection of too much. The English path is indulgent, but it is sterile to live in borrowed houses.

I can't turn my back on Oxford experience; knowledge, once tasted, can never be forgotten. I decide to leave Victorian India to cultivate her fig trees and escape to Oxford.

III | DELHI HEAT

BEFORE spending a bummy month together in India, Dom Moraes and I were great friends at Oxford. I am not quite sure what friendship means elsewhere, but at Oxford it means being able to spend a whole day together — that is, from breakfast to bedtime — and being able to roam from room to room, sometimes bumming drinks, sometimes taking along hip flasks and sharing drinks with other friends. At Oxford we worked frightfully hard perhaps for five or six days, five or six weeks, and after this intensive period we took a physical and spiritual holiday, bumming and being amiable, visiting and being visited. These bummy days were an Oxford specialty. Just as some people have Sabbaths, we had bummy days. They are necessary to those of us who lead serious lives day in and day out, like ants on the pages of a folio musty with age and use. But these were not so much days of rest as days of motion, days of looking out on life through whiskey-colored glasses, days when we spent most of our time pacing, just so we would remember how to use our legs and feet.

Both Dom and I graduated from Oxford in July, and perhaps, before I get too deeply occupied with other matters, it would be best to say a word or two about the literary set to which Dom and I belonged at Oxford. In contrast to the smart set, our literary set was always changing, like the water in the river. Sometimes it included people like a boy I'll call Elton, who, after graduating, was engaged in half-hearted research — and research at Oxford amounts to very little, especially if you have had a book or two of poems published by a respectable press. Elton was happily engaged to a very pretty girl until he unhappily discovered he was a homosexual. Sometimes our set included people like Del, who had received first-class honors in English and could therefore live off the capital of his brilliant undergraduate career. Del, although an American from the Middle West and a Midwestern university, was more English in manner and accent than most Englishmen from the South of England. Sometimes it included people like Patrick, a talented actor and an Oxford figure, sometimes it was visited by the three boys who ran the literary magazines at the university, and sometimes Jasper Griffin, a great classic at Balliol, would join us to sneer at the last piece of clever, clever writing in *Isis*. The set also had certain constant features, such as the mistresses of the littérateurs, but otherwise it was always in a state of flux. So, you see, it wasn't really a set. It was just a river of people. Because of the very nature of the river, our customs were not fixed — except, that is, between two or three friends.

Dom Moraes — like me, an Indian — was much more idle than I, but then he was a poet. He didn't have to worry about degrees and that kind of thing. A small book of poems of his, *A Beginning*, had been a triumphant success. His poetry was highly personal, sensuous, and filled with what one critic termed "rapturous ironies." He wrote like Dylan Thomas, he was lovable like Thomas, and like Thomas he was a lady's man. In our talk, Dom and I often attached "kins" to words. We liked the words better that way. Perhaps it was a remnant of pig Latin, but we thought of it as somehow Socratic. Of course, we couldn't really explain it at all. When we were both drunk (Domkins more than mekins), we attached "kins" to practically everything. It was just more bummy and more comradely. We also had a habit of putting "little" and "tiny" in front of words. For example, one of us might say to the other, "Let us go and see our little friend," or "Let us go and see our tiny friend." Now, "little friend" and "tiny friend" most of the time, though not always, referred to young ladies, but we called them "little friend" and "tiny friend" not because they were Lolitas but simply because the words "little" and "tiny" gave, we thought, more rhythm to our speech and, anyway, made it characteristically our own, as opposed to everyone else's. There were many other nuances of speech and habit in our friendship. For instance, we seldom told an unvarnished truth; we made whatever happened to us more fanciful and funny, to amuse ourselves and our friends. (In this Dom was more gifted than I, but he brought out my playful self.) This was not necessarily intentional. It was just part of our natures, or perhaps, more accurately, it was an escape from our natures. Both of us wore heavy armor, and our nonsense shielded us from the public, and from each other, and from ourselves. This is, in fact, to say that the friendship between Dom and me was English — reserved, witty, sarcastic, intellectual, and sometimes uncommunicative, if you took words alone as an index of feelings. But perhaps I've said enough to give some hint of the background to our summer month in India.

In New Delhi, I feel stranded — heat, sunstroke,

flies, and starving millions. I have been away from
India and living in America and England too long.
I have spent weeks getting reacquainted with the
country and my family. I have traveled through villages, I have sat for hours listening to politicians and
religious leaders, I have talked with strangers on the
street. This, I am told, is part of my education; it
is very necessary — in fact, morally obligatory. I am
saddened by the unhappiness around me. It is over-
whelming; everyone says, and I agree, that this
is because I am unable to keep my wits about me,
having been away so long. Everyone advises a fur-
lough.

The telephone rings and penetrates the educative
process. "This is me!" says a voice. "Hello, it's you,
on the phonekins," I reply, and Oxford is in India.
Adolescence all over again. Fun all over again. Dom,
who has followed his father to New Delhi, has
spent some weeks in Bombay doing much the same
thing I have been doing, so he, too, needs a fur-
lough. He settles into a room in a posh hotel, and
fills the cabinet with nectar — drinks for him and
tiny drinks for me. We get together — a bummy
Oxford surprise. First thing we do after some drinking is to go to the Volga, a bourgeois Delhi place
with upper-class pretensions. Dom is slightly un-
manageable. I order a four-course dinner. Dom says

he wants nothing to eat, but I say he must eat, because liquids without solids are bad for the health. So I order for him. Dom speaks only English, for though he was brought up in Bombay, he's had much less Indian background than I. I am at home in three Indian languages and so can order conveniently. Dom accidentally splashes soup on my suit, then feeds a tiny bit of rice to imaginary dogs under the table. I am embarrassed but enjoy being the center of attention. A Sikh at the far left table picks up the phone, dials a number, then tries, in Punjabi, to persuade someone to come to the Volga immediately. "You can't imagine what is going on here," he says. "Just come for five minutes." (The fool doesn't realize that I can understand Punjabi.) Dom then feeds a tiny bit of pudding to the imaginary dogs. The waiters don't know what to do. The orchestra starts playing conservative English melodies as loudly and furiously as possible. We stagger out, to everyone's relief, and get a taxi and order the driver to take us to my home.

Dom tries to give his whole bankroll to the taxi driver for his kind services. The taxi driver thanks him profusely, but I insist that Dom doesn't really want to do this. "But I do," he says, and the taxi driver believes him. I intervene, and save the money and the situation by taking Dom into the house.

Next morning, Dom is up early. "Bad influence of gin," he says. "Scotch is much better, gives you longer sleep." I breakfast, but Dom does not. We explain to the family that he is not hungry.

We wander out into the streets and are soon choking with dust, heat, and lack of direction. Who are the great literary people in Delhi? We cannot think of many. We head for the house of Khushwant Singh, a Sikh novelist and translator of English. We catch him unawares — nothing on his head, and his hair covering his face — but he hides his surprise and expresses his delight. His thick, long hair makes him look like a scarecrow from the back. He puts on a turban and seems at once genuinely pleased to see us. He wants to do an article on Dom, make him better known in India. We discuss the possibilities for a great Indian novel. Both Dom and I make fatuous remarks, but Khushwant says it is possible to have a great Indian novel in English. We heckle him, and he adores it. We think he's wonderful: large and tall; lecherous eyes; open face and open humor; beard covering his Adam's apple. He talks in a colloquial Punjabi, like a villager just come to town. But as soon as he speaks English he becomes a sophisticate at St. James's.

From Khushwant's we go to Narayana Menon's. Menon is magnificent: tall and lean; bright eyes;

pipe; wonderfully long, delicate fingers; manners like Del's; five years' experience at the B.B.C.; a book on Yeats; the sensibilities and responsiveness of a musician. He plays us a beautiful southern melody on an Indian instrument. He plucks it lovingly. There is something very artistic about the atmosphere — wicker chairs, great paintings by Hussain and Jamini Roy on the walls, the room filled with books — and his little daughter wants autographs. We thumb through the pages of her autograph book. The book seems to include signatures of all the great writers who have visited India in the last five years, plus those of all the Indian painters. Narayana says he left the B.B.C., on a wave of enthusiasm for independence, to join All India Radio, and now thinks it was a great mistake. Bureaucracy is immobile and trying, and does not allow him to do creative programs such as he could do on the Third. He is robbed of English happiness. Narayana becomes our mentor. All of a sudden, Delhi begins to smile. The heat is no longer like kilns but like animals. We drink beer in mugs; after each fill we say "Cheers," and we talk of Michelangelo and Yehudi Menuhin and Oxford. It seems we are smoking the fag end of an Oxford cigarette.

That afternoon, Dom and I accept an invitation to go to All India Radio. Dom plays hard to get. Says

he's leaving for Russia tomorrow. If they want him
to read his poems, he must have the studio that very
minute. He throws the whole machine out of gear.
The All India Radio people are eager to have both
of us interviewed, but we can't think of a subject.
We want to chat and gossip. They wish for something more definite. They ask us whether we want
to be interviewed by somebody. So we have the
director ring up Khushwant. Khushwant is sleeping, but we have him awakened. He says he won't
come in a taxi, even though the director will pay
the cost. He wants a special All India limousine sent
for him. Some more telephoning, and a V.I.P.
limousine goes for Khushwant. We get a studio
and perform individually, and then Khushwant interviews us. Then some more discussions, and quarrels with the director. But strangely, by the end
of the afternoon they like us. They cannot say why;
perhaps it's because we are different. We come
away from All India Radio pleased with ourselves.
It is evening.

Evenings are a problem in Delhi, so we ask the
taxi driver about "entertainment." He giggles mali-
ciously, looks back at our faces and clothes, and
then removes the evil smirk from his face. "The best

night club is in that hotel around the corner," he says.

"Can we drink there?" Dom asks.

"There is no drink and no cabaret in Delhi — that is, in public," the taxi driver says.

"What shall we do there?" I ask, and the smirk returns.

We discover he's a pimp. "If you really want to hear some singing and see some good dancing . . ."

I understand, but Dom does not, because, as I've said, he was brought up in a very English atmosphere (his father is from Goa and is an Oxford graduate) and can't speak a word of any native language. He thinks this a good thing, because he writes his poetry in English. I tell Dom about the driver's suggestion. He breaks into a long laugh, and I really think the driver is hurt, or perhaps believes he has made a mistake, because he says nothing more. We go on to Dom's room, and I have a drink and he has drinks. But there's still nothing to do, so we wander out again and go to the very posh Gymkhana Club. It's like walking into the house of the viceroy himself; one sees his ghost stamping up and down. The club has one of the few real bars in Delhi, and the Kashmir Room, and a large, sumptuous, brocaded dining room where the orchestra plays light, frothy music and where Indian hus-

bands dance with wives, now and again shouting
"Whoopee!" in what they think is an American
way. Little children of the civil servants swim in
the swimming pool, and there are almost more bearers than members.

When we walk into the club, the head porter
can hardly understand what we say. "I never heard
anyone talk so softly! Aren't they well-mannered?"
he shouts behind us as we begin our tour of the
shadow of the British raj. (By now, Dom and I
have decided to tour our country like wandering
minstrels, reading poetry and talking.) And by and
by we come upon both our fathers, and they introduce us to two sisters and their mother. These are
delicious girls. They seem to be just out of the
health shop — pink all over, liquid eyes — and they
speak English as though they'd just come from England, though they are wearing saris. I notice that
they also speak English to the bearers, and the bearers are impressed. They have unpronounceable
names. It's hard to hear because of the noise, so Dom
and I whisper to each other, referring to our new
acquaintances as the "pink girls." Their mother is
constantly pushing them forward, until the girls are
on top of us. We notice they are terribly well-
shaped and pretty, but we can't determine their
ages. They seem eager, and we feel a bit hemmed

in and try to disappear, but we don't succeed until we have been forced to accept an invitation to tea at their home in the old city.

We go back to Dom's hotel, drink some more, and have an enormous meal brought up to our room. We eat it very hastily and nervously, because the bearers, who won't go out of the room, stare at us. We feel guilty, and we look out of the window and see somebody scrounging in the dustbins. "Ved," Dom says, "what is that line in 'Howl' — 'The best minds of my generation . . . dragging themselves through the negro streets'?" "But Dom, beats are anything but the best minds of our generation." We feel terribly depressed, and I have another drink and Dom has some more drinks. Then we start gossiping about Khushwant, the radio, and the pink girls. We note that the pinks would be good for bedkins. We note that they are different from other Indian girls in saris, who are shy and blush too easily, without cause. We think their mother is terribly sweet but a bit too aggressive. All in all, we are troubled about the pinks.

Next day brings good news — a visitor from abroad, a Canadian reporter at large, is in India. We are introduced to him at breakfast by a common acquaintance. He is dressed with Edwardian elegance suitable for a morning call at court; but his paunch, twice the size of any in the middle-class, middle-aged world, destroys the lines of his suit. His complexion is sallow, he's stubby, and he looks every bit his early forties. In our shorthand Dom and I call him the Canadian mahatma; he was Gandhi's acquaintance and has written about Mahatma and himself.

I must have copy ready for the *Statesman*, so I rush away, leaving the Canadian mahatma in Dom's charge. When I return to Dom's room for morning coffee, he tells me that after breakfast he and the Canadian mahatma went to Gandhi's grave. The mahatma, who had already started drinking, looked at the grass and the trees and said, "Where is the loincloth? Bring in the loincloth!" The pilgrims stared at him, unable to understand why an expensively dressed Canadian, bottle in hand, should require a loincloth. Taking out a large silk handkerchief, the mahatma spread it on the grass. Dom found the performance eccentric and un-understandable. The mahatma, straightening his suit, sat on his handkerchief and wept drunken tears. And then he ceremoniously stood up, leaving his improvised loincloth on the ground.

Dom continues.

"We returned to the hotel and he forced me to

recite some poems and he wept some more. I've never seen anything like it. I couldn't very well ask him why he was weeping, but after one of the poems, he said, 'The Mahatma would have wept because Mahatma liked Beauty, and I have been left the custodian of Beauty.' "

"What is all this nonsense?" I say to Dom. "You mistake me for one of your audiences."

While we talk the telephone rings and the Canadian mahatma asks us to come and help him pack. He is leaving that afternoon. Before we know it Dom and I are in a taxi going to his hotel. It is a new, fashionable hotel, one of the most expensive in Delhi. It is mainly for foreigners. It would cost the average Indian a year's income to live there a week.

We take the lift and walk through a labyrinth to reach his door. The mahatma has a bottle of whiskey in each hand.

"Have a drink," he says, and we sit down. I refuse the drink. It is only eleven-thirty in the morning.

"Shouldn't we pack first?" I ask.

"No, sit down," the mahatma says. He looks better sitting down in a chair because somehow the paunch is much less obtrusive when it is doubled up.

"I wonder if the Mahatma would have liked this

nonsense?" I whisper to Dom. Dom clears his throat uncomfortably. "You know," I continue aloud, "Mahatma used to live on three and a half annas a day."

The mahatma looks hurt and explains defensively, "It wasn't always easy to find refrigeration in primitive villages. Some days Gandhi's simple meal used to cost a couple of dollars to produce. When he was in England, goat's milk was a positive luxury."

The mahatma seems to be using dirty words in a temple. Dom clears his throat uncomfortably again. He isn't saying very much so I have to ask the questions. "What time is your plane?"

"We must lie down and think," the mahatma says.

I repeat the question.

"We must lie down and think."

The bearer comes in with some nuts. "Sahib, your plane leaves at two and last night your friend asked me to tell you that you should leave the hotel by one."

The mahatma yawns and asks for more ice.

"Perhaps, sir, we ought to help you pack," Dom says.

"Mahatma," says the Canadian mahatma, "was the greatest saint since Buddha. Gandhiji comprehended the great Indian truth — that one must be either a politician or a saint. He was both but I am neither. I am just a writer." He stops, thinks, continues, "I must lie down and think — that is what the Mahatma would have done if he had been corrupt like me."

I am exasperated. It is twelve-fifteen already. "May I call the bearer?" I ask. "He could pack for you."

The mahatma shakes his big head forcefully.

"Don't you dare do that," he says. I disregard the drunken injunction. I ring for the bearer and speak to him in Hindi. "Don't pay any attention to the sahib. Fetch the suitcase and bring out the clothes."

Ridiculous activity. The bearer drags out an old suitcase tied with hemp and the mahatma tries to make him put it back. I tell the bearer to get the clothes. The bearer shuttles from one sahib to the other, but I win and the mahatma seems reconciled.

Piles of clothes dwarf the suitcase. We look for another. The mahatma shouts, "There is no other. Gandhiji carried only one sack, I carry only one suitcase." I translate this for the bearer.

The bearer inquires how the sahib got all the clothes into the hotel. A good question, I think, and put it to the mahatma.

"I wore them on my back — can't you see I'm a rich bastard who likes to show his clothes?" I leave the bearer in his ignorance.

The mahatma fingers the piles of clothing, turns over replicas of the suit he is wearing, silk shirts with French cuffs and detachable collars, several dressing gowns. He asks the bearer through me if he wants some clothes. The answer is yes.

"Here, can you use a silk dressing gown?"

"No, Sahib, but my wife would wear it in the bazaars and bless you."

The mahatma tosses the dressing gown to the bearer.

"Shirts?"

"Yes, Sahib."

Half a dozen silk shirts join the dressing gown on the floor.

The action continues. The bearer, like a vendor, now sits in front of the suitcase. To his left is the mahatma's diminishing pile; to his right a steadily growing one, his own. He hugs it, and his face recalls the monkey in a story I knew as a child. Two cats fight over a fish, and the monkey, chosen to divide it fairly, gobbles it all. Where are the cats?

"Ask the bearer," the mahatma tells me, "what he would do if he had all these clothes."

"I would give a suit to each of my brothers. We would have a feast on the sahib's birthday and pray for him."

"How in hell do you know when my birthday
is? Anyway, I'm not worthy."

I edit his answer.

"If you like, we will wear them on Christmas."

"Is this man a Christian?" The question is directed
to me.

Yes, the bearer is a Christian convert. His whole
village in the United Province follows Jesus Christ.
The mahatma is really angry.

"Converts have no ethics. They have been corrupted. I didn't come to India to give clothes to
Christians. I must lie down and think."

Translation becomes difficult. I cannot convey
the hurt of the mahatma to the bearer or the confusion of the bearer to the mahatma.

"Damn. Wear them — wear them on Gandhiji's
birthday — or Nehru's birthday. Look — will you
swear to me to wear them on Nehru's birthday?"

The bearer swears. But when the mahatma presses
him for Nehru's birth date he becomes evasive, and
finally takes refuge behind drawn-out calculations
of the Hindu calendar. He arrives at the right day
and is rewarded with a dinner jacket.

"Wear it and let me see how it looks on you."

The bearer is embarrassed. He holds the dazzling
dinner jacket in his apron without touching it.

"He must put it on," commands the mahatma. I

prod the bearer. Finally we force him into the bathroom with the dinner jacket.

"It will be too loose for him."

"But you won't take it back, will you?" It occurs to me that this may be the mahatma's way of jesting, and I am frightened. His kindly smile reassures me.

The bearer returns. He has wrapped the jacket in a clean towel. "Let the sahib take it back."

The mahatma laughs, and flings the jacket on the bearer's pile, and pats the bearer on the back. The bearer whispers to me, "If the sahib would like to stay here another night, I could make good arrangements for him." I ignore this.

Meantime Dom has been on the telephone trying to locate the mahatma's lost books. The mahatma has spent days collecting a Sanskrit library for Canada. Dom is successful.

The mahatma has another drink on the recovered books.

The bearer makes an exasperating request. "Would the sahib please write a letter to the hotel manager to tell him that he has given the clothes to me of his own will?"

The mahatma reluctantly sits down at the table and starts to write, with a shaky hand. Each piece has to be described and initialed. He reads aloud: "Sir: I give this bearer one silk dressing gown, also six silk shirts with French cuffs, two striped shirts and one white. One dinner jacket. Two suits. . . ."

While the mahatma reads, the bearer retreats to the bathroom to return the towel. He does not come back until the list is completed. It is one-thirty. The bearer wants to carry the suitcase down but the mahatma insists on carrying it himself.

By the time we get him to a taxi he has only fifteen minutes to catch the plane. He throws his arms around us. "Boys, India is too much for me. I wish I could be Gandhiji. But I'm not a saint, just a filthy bastard."

I leave Dom and spend the rest of the day quietly at home.

Next morning, we are back at Khushwant's, but this time we sip tea, and Khushwant has a headdress on before we arrive. He seems to have had a premonition about our restless wanderings. He's extremely amusing. He says he has written his fifth book and titled it something like *I Shall Not Be a Nightingale;* he thinks it will sell like *Lolita*, which is, however, an immoral book, because since reading it he has become overconscious of the friends of his thirteen-year-old daughter, especially when he sees them around the swimming pool. Khushwant says that from five to seven every morning he has a Sikh priest come and visit him to take him through the ancient Sikh scriptures.

We lunch with Narayana, and I think, from the way he holds his silver, that he is an artist to his fingertips. Dom asks him if he's heard of the pink girls. "The older sister," Narayana tells us, "worked in the theater, and sometimes her work was at night. To avoid incidents, she was given a driver and escort. In fact, it amounted to two drivers, who watched each other. Door-to-door service, you know. Safe, secure, and very necessary in a place like Delhi — indeed, throughout India. Well, one night she worked until two-thirty, and as she was going from the theater to the car, there were loud screams in the corridor, and within a matter of seconds a crowd had collected. She shouted accusations of intended rape. Many of the theater people ran down the corridor on a man-chase, but the assailant had too much of a head start. A chance police car hunted him down. He claimed to be innocent, but he admitted being in the building on a friendly visit. He would not disclose the name of the friend, and since the evidence was circumstantial, the girl was advised to drop the case. But the mother wanted the man hanged, drawn, and quartered, and the older of your little pinks claimed to have met the fate of the heroine of *A Passage to India*. The theater building became Marabar Caves. In the courtroom it seemed that the girl and the accused knew each other. One person had seen them at the pictures together, and also there was the matter of returning a book to the girl, which this gentleman had overlooked. Naturally, the question: What book, borrowed when? It was a farce." Narayana counsels us to beware of these girls, and not to court them in the Western style. If we hold hands with them, we should be prepared for a breach-of-promise suit. We are frightened and alarmed and we tremble at the prospect of going to tea with them the next day.

In the evening we wander into a very rich neighborhood looking for a lady known to us as Miss Fulbright Fellowship. Khushwant has told us about her. "The quietest, gentlest soul walking in Delhi. Beauty and loveliness. But my name will be no recommendation for you." There had been a New Year's dance at the Golf Club, the smartest society represented. Khushwant had suggested the dance and made the arrangements. Guests were asked to bring bottles of whiskey; and since many of them were in the military or diplomatic service they had access to tax-free liquor. Some brought as much as a case. Everyone heavily drank the New Year in — dancing, rollicking, rocking with delight. There were lots of leftovers and Khushwant was rewarded for his exertions with the unopened bottles. He was able to stock his cabinet with liquor for the following six months. This was a reason, among others, for his being the center of Delhi society.

By the time Khushwant saw Miss Fulbright standing in a corner looking on at the party, he was high and merry. He thought she was moody. The hapless Khushwant rushed over to Miss Fulbright, gathered her in his arms, and began dancing.

"I can't dance! I can't dance!" insisted Miss Fulbright.

Khushwant thought she was being shy, so he dragged her across the floor, back and around. When he stopped to catch his breath he noticed her face tense with pain and realized she was lame. For Khushwant the party was finished.

He lost Miss Fulbright as a friend, and she avoided him like a woman who has been roughly handled. But whatever her judgment on Khushwant, he nursed only delicate thoughts about her. As he told us about the party he blushed behind his big beard.

We cannot find Miss Fulbright. The street she lives on is strange. It has no order. The numbers of the houses leap from tens to hundreds, and it seems everyone has posted his lucky number on the door. The houses on the street are large and the numbers printed on them are larger. When we finally reach her house, having had three wrong doors shut on us, we find a quietness and eloquence which we have never quite associated with foreigners in India.

The room is air-conditioned but the machine, unlike those in less expensive houses, is far away; we can't hear the motor rumbling.

Miss Fulbright sits on a large sofa but somehow makes it small. She serves us small glasses of Dubonnet, which we sip. The conversation gets quieter and quieter until all three of us are whispering, missing each other's remarks but somehow feeling happy in each other's company. She is excited about a project to use bullocks for generating electricity. "Wouldn't it be magnificent if the bullocks, which are idle during the winter, could be used to produce electricity half the year!" "Is it successful? Have you tried it?"

"We have in a few villages," replies Miss Fulbright. "The bullocks keep in shape for the harvest and don't become lazy; villages get electricity without burning coal, and all the children turn out to watch the bullocks go round and round to light the lamps. I saw it some time ago and loved it. It was Indian and beautiful."

"But," I say, "the real need for electricity is during harvest time."

Dom says, "But surely bullocks are temperamental and will not move like dynamos."

And I ask, "But how can you store electricity?"

Miss Fulbright says, "Oh, but this is the romance of the bullocks! This is the great thing for India. It uses the natural resources of the country. It also preserves the village community. Gandhiji would have liked that."

There is something about the way she says things that makes the ridiculous convincing.

A friend of Miss Fulbright drops in. He is an aged professor of Sanskrit — simple, sedate, scholarly but not scholarly in an ordinary way. He recites Sanskrit poetry and makes us forget the time and the place. "The poetry I am reciting to you," he says, "is something which may have been recited on the banks of the Ganges two thousand years ago — with exactly the same intonation, the same accent. The language has been preserved not on paper but in the hearts and minds of the people. Today you could go to Haridwar or Benares and hear Brahmins reciting Sanskrit poetry as though time had never moved."

I feel slightly uncomfortable when Miss Fulbright speaks English after his recitation. The English jars. But Miss Fulbright and the Sanskrit professor seem to share quiet simplicity. They are less divided from each other by language and generations than most English from Indians. Somehow Miss Fulbright seems to belong to India.

The bearer comes in and turns out the lights. Only candles are left burning. We can tell by the way she smiles at the professor that she is in love with Sanskrit; Sanskrit is in her eyes. I suspect a romance. We all end up reciting poetry to each other. When we leave, we leave behind us a beautiful evening.

Dom says in the taxi, "What a romance!"

"You mean the bullocks?" I say.

"No, theirs."

"Dom, it couldn't be more impractical than the bullock experiment."

Dom says, "But it couldn't be lovelier, either," and we laugh, and then think of Khushwant taking this dainty creature into his muscular grip.

The next day we pass the time with college friends of my sister — taking snapshots, talking art, and drinking coffee nervously until, full of trepidation, we go to tea with the pinks. Thank God for the mother. She settles down in the room.

There is also a third visitor, a general, who talks with the mother. The pink girls call him General, and the general is angry and puzzled. "Why this big change?" he asks. "Until yesterday, you called me Uncle. Why General today?"

"General, General, General," says the younger pink defiantly. "General, General, General. I'm grown up now."

"You are a slip of a girl," says the general.

The younger pink puffs her mouth. The mother gestures, and the general is quiet. The older pink gets up and comes and practically sits on Dom's lap, and then says, "Excuse me."

We discover that the younger pink is still in a convent school, so we ask how old she is. She pouts. We drop the question.

The younger pink talks big. "I hate nuns," she says.

"Don't be silly," says the older pink.

"I go out every evening," the younger pink says, "and stay out until three o'clock."

The older pink says that this is wrong, and that she should recognize the importance of education.

The mother disappears, and the general, after bending down and giving both the girls a hug, goes away also.

"Do you write?" I ask the older pink.

"Oh, just now and then, for a gossip magazine," the younger pink answers for her. "If you come to a party, she will include you in her list."

76

Delhi Heat

As the conversation progresses — or, rather, as the two sisters talk — the small, tidy sitting room becomes peopled with their shrill friends. They are the smart set, and all seem to be beautiful, gay, provocative — full of sex and charm. They all seem to love music, dancing, and our two pink friends.

Teatime expires. Anyway, it is hot and tedious, so we try to get away. But the girls stop us. "Stay for drinks," they say. And we do. Our spirits are considerably dampened when the servant dances in with a trayful of warm Coca-Colas. We drink the tepid drink. The conversation seems, finally, to have nothing put pauses. The girls won't let us leave them that evening without fixing a time to return.

In the taxi we swear to each other never again. "We don't belong in that smart set," I say, and Dom says, "but maybe we *need* pink girls. Or publicity agents. Or pink clouds. Or something," and we laugh. "We need publicity agents," I say, "and little pink clouds too?" "Do we need pink clouds, Vedkins?" "Better than pink girls," and we laugh.

Next day we find ourselves at Delhi University. Dom and I have taken to speaking at colleges. Our performances are uneven and this is partly due to our moodiness and partly to the variety of groups we have to read to and address. You see, everything in India is vague. You may get a telephone call in

77

the morning with an invitation from a college, but until you arrive, it is impossible to know whether the audience will be composed of staff, students, or bystanders.

Once I spoke at a woman's college. The principal requested me to speak softly because the hall had hidden microphones and perfect loudspeakers, and after I finished the one-hour lecture on American universities, I discovered that no one could hear me because the Delhi Electric Company had switched off the current, a usual method for replacing parts or saving electricity. The principal was proud of the girls, who were so well trained that, even though they couldn't hear a word, they pretended to hear and understand. "In England the audience would have thrown tomatoes or at least shouted," I said to the principal, but she said ironically, "There is no heckling in Indian colleges, we have only hunger strikes."

We have come to expect surprises during our speaking engagements.

When we turn up at Delhi University, we can't find the lecture hall. A dashing young man comes up to us and presents himself as a reporter. "Do you know where Mr. Mehta and Mr. Moraes are speaking?" We introduce ourselves and together look for the hall. The meeting has started without us. The

occasion is the anniversary of the English Union
or some such, and a wiry, nervous professor is
lecturing on the virtues of English language and
literature. His introductory speech for us becomes
a paean on English: "Like everything in India,
standards of teaching English are declining even
though English is five times a better language than
Hindi because English has five times the vocabulary
of Hindi, yet no Indian can write decent prose in
English or Hindi because, in the first case, the language isn't refined and, in the second case, students
have stopped studying the great masters of English
prose — Chaucer, Shakespeare, Milton, Johnson,
Molière, Goethe, Tolstoy." The professor appears
confused, and he looks at his notes once again and
asks the students, who are busily writing, to elimi-
nate the name of Tolstoy. "As I was saying," he
goes on, "the study of English has much to recommend itself and I do not mean only the study of
words but study of literature, for the learning of
language is simply a means to an end and we must
never lose sight of the end for end is everything.
But that is not to say means are unimportant, for
if that were so, there would be no end. I hope
my meaning is clear." After his lecture, we see that
many heads in the audience are nodding and some
desertions have begun from the back row. The

wiry, nervous professor finally looks up from his notes towards us. "I want to now introduce you to literature which Mr. Moraes and Mr. Mehta have brought to us," and he breaks the back of yet another sentence. "On second thought," he continues, "I will let them be introduced by themselves as I do not wish to presume, and besides . . ." and so on and so forth.

I come alive with the poems of Dom. He reads them in a quick and hurried way as though he was reading words he didn't understand, words which belonged to another language. Now and again, I detect a sort of irony in his voice and find him parroting his own poems. The audience, however, is attentively serious.

After Dom, I speak on fact and fancy and tell them about an English professor of mine who preferred fancies to facts, a novel to a history book, his eleven o'clock cup of coffee with gossip to the morning newspaper. "The world," he used to say, "is a shoddy place, and no one can endure reality for long. We must all have escapes from the world and refresh ourselves at the burning fountain of literature. Man can transcend his infinitesimal experience only through imagination."

I talk about beauty and recite verses and passages. Dom joins me in conjuring beauty and recites

verses from poets past, present. It is great fun, sometimes a tiny bit bizarre because there are tiny laughs
from the audience when we begin a quotation and
can't finish. Afterward there is tea outside, and tea
in India means a sort of supper, enormous quan-
tities of food — hot, spiced, pickled. Undergrad-
uates eat with their hands and suck their fingers
clean. Every student turns out to be an amateur
palmist and they fight for our hands. Two palmists
win the scrimmage because of their superior age.
They hold our hands in their palms and finger them
as though they were kneading dough. The students
sit around us in a circle on the grass. Dom's hand is
read first. "You are poet to your fingertips," it is
announced. "You will cross the seven seas seven
times, you will have seven children, you will not
always be happy." He is to live to be seventy-seven.

Dom says he would rather have seven wives and
the death of Dylan Thomas. That sort of death is
more poetic. My hand is read and commented upon,
but by the time my turn comes everyone is reading
each other's hands.

The possessive pinks turn up to drag us away.
They are free with their compliments about our
speeches (they smuggled themselves into the audience); they treat us like their little protectorates
and try to protect us from being mobbed.

Walking the Indian Streets

They discourage students from being overfriendly with us and turn them from palmistry to horoscopes. By the end of tea we are left with the prospect of spending another evening with the pinks. But Dom and I get lost in a vanishing act.

We lunch with Khushwant the next day. Lots and lots of Americans are there. A tall American girl, who is an adviser on manure, says Dom has the most beautiful face she's ever seen. Dom clears his throat two or three times, as he usually does when he's flattered, and doesn't know what to do with his hands. It's a strange lunch, for the Americans talk terribly loud; we get the impression that some of the Americans in India are a mistake, but, of course, there's no way to test this. A queue of rats slides into a corner hole during the lunch. We don't feel hungry. We tease Khushwant about the rats, and he says they're a Delhi occurrence, and reminds us we are in India. We tell him about our pink girls, and then we try to be clever, and call their parlor the pink-light district. Khushwant says he knows them, and says they are innocent but pretty. During part of the lunch, Khushwant sits on the floor and drinks beer and grips the arm of a very fat American girl, and she says she will report him to the F.B.I. for having bad fingerprints. Khushwant laughs, but we

82

don't think it's a frightfully good joke. We notice
he doesn't let go of the arm, and his enormously attractive bearded face is turned up to the girl.

The ladies disappear into the bedroom, and Khushwant tells us an amusing story. During the war, he
was forced by a group of men to go with them to a
red-light district to keep them company. There he
found six girls playing a very curious game with
one G.I. They were kicking an old tin of boot polish
from one side of the veranda to the other. The girls
and the G.I. were breathless. Two girls, Khushwant,
and the G.I. were left on the veranda after certain
arrangements had been made among the others. And
Khushwant, having only a "writer's interest" in going to the district, paced up and down nervously
until the G.I. resumed his game and invited Khushwant to join, and there he was, kicking an old tin of
boot polish around the veranda with two girls and a
G.I., while the other men were with the girls inside.
"Very, very tough game," Khushwant told us. "I
was breathless, too, after fifteen minutes. After the
game, one of the girls told me that they had tried
everything to entice the G.I. He had been coming
there for the last nine months, but he wanted nothing at all. He just wanted to play that game." Perhaps in India the pink cloud was a boot-polish tin.
It was a thoroughly strange lunch.

Walking the Indian Streets

Indeed, everything we did in India was strange. Or at least we thought it strange. Dom and I would entertain each other and whoever was with us by saying, for example, "Khushwant's lunch was very strange." It was a wonderful opening, giving us an opportunity to embellish and embroider little incidents. This was done not only to amuse our company with fantastically exaggerated accounts but somehow to find an escape from our own gloom.

We see a lot of the pinks. For one thing, there is nothing else to do, and, for another, while they are extremely boring to be with, in their absence they provide us with little rapturous ironies. One day we arrive at the pinks' place in a merry state. We want to relieve ourselves. They lock their lavatory doors. We can't understand for what reasons. They seem to be embarrassed for us to see any part of their small house. So we get in a taxi and look for Gents. We go to a nearby hotel and they practically come to the Gents door with us, still unbelieving and unwilling to let us get out of their sight. We almost collapse in the Gents with laughter and speculate about the pink lavatory — probably an outhouse. The girls haven't had any dinner, so the four of us go to the Volga looking for sandwiches. We're turned away, so we go to Gaylord's and get the girls some sandwiches and try to give them the slip. They will not accept excuses. All of us get into a taxi, and the girls help us look for a patch of grass, because Mother is expected home. We find a patch of grass, and while the girls unwrap the sandwiches we ask the taxi driver to join us and give him some sandwiches. The girls are hurt at our "democratic" hobnobbing and talk in pig Latin about their disapproval. I have the embarrassing task of getting rid of the driver. I ask him to move the car, please. He, in turn, is hurt at the hint. We take a little walk, but the patch of grass is anything but exclusive. We stumble over some people. The air is cut with laughter and screams. The girls say they are sexual screams. We are frightened by the unknown, and hurry back to the car and the protection of the driver. The girls lecture us about the social advantages of Delhi, about making our homes in India, about the convenience of servants. Oh, the life is gay, social, and wonderful, but we feel depressed.

Dom says he can't write any poetry in India, so he must leave for England. I can't write either. We begin to stay more and more in Dom's room, and come to love the rattle of ice in glasses, the whiff of strong drinks. We eat little and cover up the windowpanes with shades. The pinks ring up eight times a day, but we pretend to be busy with our poems and novels.

Walking the Indian Streets

We go to Narayana. He consoles us, and says perhaps we would enjoy seeing a man I choose to name Mr. Chatterji. He has been to England, though only for a few weeks, and yet manages to live and write in India. "He lives by the old Delhi wall," Narayana says. "One of the most successful Indian prose writers — disliked in India, loved in England."

"What's his address?" I ask.

"Don't know," Narayana says. "Just ask for the Bengali babu [gentleman]."

So we hail a taxi and ask to go to the Delhi wall — a slum area, like the East End in London or the lower East Side in New York, except that here the poverty is just plain horrid, naked on the streets. We ask a great many little children about the famous writer. They disclaim any knowledge of him. We describe him as a man of sixty, and a child pipes up, "I've never heard of anyone so old in this part." Laughter around us. We walk up and down the narrow gullies, in and out of small, stablelike houses, but no Mr.Chatterji. "Oh, yes, I think I know him," somebody says. "Isn't he the one who goes to universities with a cloth bag, tall and handsome?" We pass on. Finally, we remember Narayana's advice about asking for the Bengali babu instead of Mr. Chatterji. We are directed to a rickety staircase — up one flight, up two flights, up three flights. We say the magic words "Bengali babu," and we are directed to go left. A shriveled-up, naked figure is sprawled out on the veranda. We take him for a servant of the great writer.

"Where is the sahib?" I ask.

The figure first squints, then looks at us, then points down the veranda. A second naked figure leads us down the veranda and shows us into the Bengali babu's drawing room. Two chairs, placed between two doors, catch the breeze in this room. The Bengali babu has no fan. We occupy them, grow uneasy with waiting. Then the Bengali babu, the first naked figure we saw, now dressed, appears. He majestically sits down on the floor. "The man who showed you here was my son," he says. "My other son is studying in London."

We have met many eccentrics before, but never one so eccentric as this. He lectures us about the inaccuracy of *A Passage to India* (Mr. Forster got the caste of the assize wrong). He calls us the children of darkness (without explanation). He says he knows more about English literature than anyone else in the world. "All my friends are foreigners," he says. "Indians don't like me because I think. They want to crucify me. They call me a dog who wags his tail at the smell of London stew. I am so famous, and yet no Indian of my age has visited me. Khushwant

and Narayana are exceptions. I get invited to two
hundred diplomatic cocktail parties in a season, but
I hate them, so I go to only seventy. I live here because it's the most Indian and most historic place in
the world. I'm loved by the people of the old wall."
He offers us coffee after an hour and a half of talk.
I think we pity him more than like him. We invite
him to lunch the next day and dinner the day after.
We quote him eagerly. He is an Indian writer who
can write in India; he is our hope in that darkened
sky.

At lunch the next day, Mr. Chatterji shows an
encyclopedic knowledge of English literature and
geography and people. Strange, I think, to love England as he does and yet to have spent only a few
weeks there. Strange, too, that he knows more about
England than most Englishmen. It is sad that Mr.
Chatterji should think of England as Christians
think of God — without the mystical experience.
Dom says, "England is Mr. Chatterji's pink cloud,
but his England is not ours."

One morning the darkness lifts and the face of
the sun peers through the clouds. Han Suyin is in
town. A week in America, one television interview,
and she cut short her visit by a month and came
to Delhi. "Before you die," she says, "you must
see Katmandu." Katmandu is, of course, the capital

of Nepal. Feeling close to death, we decide to go
to Nepal. Dom's father knows a general who lives
there and in whose palace we can stay. The general
is a Class A Rana. His family is second only to that
of the King of Nepal, and up until a few years back,
when there was a revolution, provided the country's
Prime Ministers.

Khushwant, Narayana, and Han Suyin make
Delhi for us, and we — Dom and I — make Delhi
for each other. I remember the last conversation —
tipsy and disorganized — with the pinks.

DOM: "The Dalai Lama awaits us."

ME: "Hum."

DOM: "We must go."

ME: "Yes, Dom."

THE PINKS: "Never, never, never, never, never."

DOM: "We must. The Dalai Lama awaits us."

ME: "After that, a plane to Katmandu."

THE PINKS: "We are coming with you."

ME: "We need them but we cannot afford them."

DOM: "Shall we go? What is the time?"

ME: "Late."

THE PINKS: "Not yet, please."

ME: "We must."

DOM: "We must. The tiny Dalai Lama awaits us,
and then a tiny plane to Katmandu, then guests of
tiny general living in tiny palace, tiny drinks, per-

haps girlkins, tiny girlkins, tiny Nepalese girlkins. The Dalai Lama awaits us."

We get up. We are pushed back into our seats. We get up again, are bounced back into our seats. Tiny tears glisten in pink eyes. We discover that younger pink is only fifteen. She goes into the bedroom, sulking, so we can't leave. A half hour of comforting.

ME: "We are late for the Dalai Lama."

THE YOUNGER PINK: "Dalai Lama, Dalai Lama, Dalai Lama! What is he to you? What are you to him?"

DOM: "A little appointment with him tomorrow."

THE YOUNGER PINK: "Tomorrow, tomorrow, tomorrow! But now it is today."

ME: "Need a good sleep."

The girls are angry. We promise to come back, before Nepal. No wet pink good-bys. Just departure. Another taxi, and we cut through the stifling air.

IV | INDIAN SUMMER

NEXT MORNING, we get into a tiny DC-3 and climb up to six thousand feet. First stop, Agra — the Taj Mahal seen through the haze from two thousand feet. Then Benares — rather pleasant. We get V.I.P. treatment. Invariably people recognize Dom or me. We are seated and served coffee. Other passengers stand in queue. We wait at the airport for six hours. The stop is supposed to be only half an hour, but the weather is bad — monsoons. The clouds gurgle and thunder. The sky is all right for a Super-Constellation but bad for a DC-3. Finally, the airline people are discouraged. The flight is postponed, and toward evening Dom and I taxi to Clark's Hotel. The rooms are a present from the airline. Benares is the oldest city in the world, and when we pass the shops, they really seem like museums. Very fat shopkeepers sit in small shops, selling antiquities, haggling. They surprise us because they sit in front of their merchandise and hide it, like tourists obscuring museum treasures. The rooms in our hotel are like those of official resthouses — flats set behind vast verandas, which take the place of corridors. We feel frustrated, and are not in the mood for a tour. A bearer asks us whether we would like a gay night. We say no and order some whiskey. Dom takes his first drink in eight hours and finishes it in a long gulp. I begin to feel sick with waiting for the plane.

We pass the evening in the bar, talking to the Indian pilot of the plane, who deplores the DC-3. He hates the monsoons. The pilot says, "God is really capricious, diabolical. If we have too much rain, we have floods, because of the mountains; if we have too little rain, we have famine. Rain or no rain, if we have clouds, we can't fly. If there are no clouds, we have sunstroke. The Hindu god is capricious. Why can't we have the spring of the Englishman and the autumn of the American? I have flown big Super-Constellations to London, and you have to see an English spring to believe it. All the kingdom of flowers smiles at you, and you feel in harmony. India is a rotten country. It has mountains, and the beauty of the mountains does delight the soul, but the mountains are the cause of the floods. It breaks my heart." The pilot spits in his beer glass.

We ask him if he would like some whiskey.

"No, thank you," he says.

"Don't you like whiskey?" Dom asks.

"I love it," the pilot says.

"Then why not have some?" I say.

"In India I never touch whiskey," he says. "It's immoral. Too much poverty. It's like drinking blood."

Dom looks away. I pick up my glass and feel very sick at my stomach.

The pilot laughs a jolly laugh and says we are both very young. He thanks us kindly and says his good nights. Both of us go to bed soon afterward.

The next morning, we spring out of bed and run to the air office and then to the airport. The voice on the loudspeaker says, "There is a break in the clouds, and we shall be flying in half an hour." We are soon up in the air, flying toward Katmandu. We sleep. Patna — last stop in India — is announced. We stroll out, then go back to the DC-3. As the plane bumps its way toward Katmandu, we reminisce about Han Suyin. She told us, "Katmandu is the most beautiful place in the world. It is a baptism of beauty. All the citizens of Katmandu are initiates into the cult of beauty, the cult of art, the cult of the gods." Dom's father called the general we are about to visit a "gay sea dog," and in our imagination we see him quilted in whiskey, women, and happiness. We bump and bounce into the valley, and we step majestically off the plane singing "Kat-man-du."

We experience a thrill as "Katmandu" is stamped on our passports. The general's chauffeur has met us at the airport. As we get into the car, we ask him what there is in Katmandu. What is the mystery and magic of Katmandu? What is its poetry? He says, "There is not much here to see. Most tourists come for the temples. It's a boring place." In English, Dom and I talk of people with drab imaginations. Majestically, superciliously, we drive toward the palace. It is like waking in a dream — sun on Katmandu, high walls of mountain, valley tucked in like a pocket of bliss, peaks all around us. No fog, no dust, no clouds — beautiful, balmy weather. We reach the general's palace, which seems to occupy almost half of Katmandu. We pass through enormous halls. On the walls all the generals of the world, all in Nepalese dress, seem to be queueing up for God knows what. Cathedral ceilings, velvet, antique furniture, ornaments, chandeliers, dimensionless — this is the palace.

We are shown to a drawing room and a sofa. We seem to be buried in satin cushions. We sink back and wait for the general. Instead, the queen of the house appears, elderly but preserved like a girl of

eighteen. Only graying hair gives away her secret.
She speaks to us in a strange tongue, and about
strange, mysterious things. She seems to be apologiz-
ing for something. Finally we are shown to our palace apartment. Five rooms. Each of our beds can
hold a half-dozen people, and the mosquito net
around it seems to enclose a secret world.

A son of the general is our host at tea. Eighteenth-
century cutlery, delicate omelets, purées, and pas-
tries. It is a perfect blend of East and West, of big
and small. The whole palace is a brocaded simplicity. No paradoxes but only riddles. Nice little tiny
lovely riddles. The son, who is about twenty and
speaks English, tells us that in Nepal, before the
revolution of 1950, "general" was an inherited title;
with Sandhurst irony and English wit, he tells us
that most of the generals have sunken cheeks and
broken backs, and that since Nepal is a peaceful
country most of the fighting is done in bed. We
finish our tea and go back to our bedroom and look
expectantly under the mosquito net and between the
white sheets. There are no visible concubines. The
servant unpacks our tiny bags and asks us if more
are coming. He wants to lay out our dinner jackets.
We have only hiking clothes — a couple of khaki
shirts and some tatty trousers.

We are summoned to dinner. There are many

other guests. The general welcomes us summarily, makes us feel that it is a great privilege even to be spoken to. We repeat our names many times, but he never gets them. There are stares from the other guests because of our clothes and shabby appearance. They seem to be insulted. The family seems huge. At least five sons are at the table, with their wives. I learn that all five of them lived in the palace and ran the politics of Nepal with their father before the revolution. I learn that the palace is equipped with its own bank, tailor, goldsmith, and watchmaker, and with a hundred servants. During coffee, I corner the general to ask him about the revolution.

"Wasn't there a revolution in Nepal a few years back?" I ask naively.

"It was the time when I lost my hundred and fifty concubines," he answers.

New definition of revolution, I think. "What happened during the revolution?" "I lost my concubines."

Before the revolution, a Rana could ride his elephant, and all the women in Katmandu would crowd onto their balconies, eager for his attentions. If he waved at one, her fortune was made. She was taken into the palace. "No elephant rides now," he says. "The good old times are over. Now I have only seventy-eight maidservants."

I go off and whisper this fact to Dom, and we approach the general together. I begin, "You see, sir, most of our life has been spent abroad and we've never met a concubine. Do you think it would be possible to meet one now?"

Dom breaks in. "The B.B.C.," he says, in a Dom-like gambit, "asked us to interview a few concubines in Nepal."

Three minutes' unnerving silence. Then the general announces militarily, "If you have any ideas about prowling around tonight, we have five Tibetan wolfhounds in the compounds." With that he contemptuously gestures our dismissal.

Days in Katmandu are, for us, days of waking. We see strange things. The strangest of all is the naturalness of the surroundings and the people. Men and women work side by side in the fields. They sing and dance with their ids but are not embarrassed. The women are beautiful and healthy, and not, like Indian women, always pulling the folds of their saris to give them more drape. The sari is the winding sheet of sex in India, but not here. And here people are not made ugly by their poverty. For the first time since we came home, it really feels as though we were on a pink cloud.

A newspaper reporter, a friend of Dom's father, is our guide through Katmandu and Nepal. By his friends he is nicknamed "Prince," because he knows every stone in Nepal. He has keys to all the secret doors that open into mysterious places. He hires us a jeep, and our first visit is to the Indian ambassador in Nepal. He is surrounded with generals and military attachés, diplomats, secretaries, but he talks to me without the pomp I have come to associate with Indian officials. He sits on his veranda holding his pipe like a pencil and now and then casually puts it up to his lips. But under his delicacy I sense the rugged wit of the mountaineers.

We discover that Han Suyin is a close friend of his. While writing her book, *The Mountain Is Young*, she lived in the Royal Palace Hotel. The ambassador gossips about her kindly. "Would you like to see her in stone?" he asks us, and leads us into his lavish drawing room. There are hardly any pictures on the walls, but all around the room there are squatting faces imprisoned in stone trying to free themselves. On one side there are the famous Ranas, half carved, some of them peering out of stony eyes. On another side, beautifully carved famous concubines. The ambassador classifies the concubines as A, B, C. Dom and I feel confused because in many instances the C concubines appear to be a better sculpture — more youthful and more beautiful than the other classes, and we can't imagine why the ambassador doesn't give himself alphas for these. He laughs when we ask him about his ranking system. "I am not classifying my own sculptures. This is the way the Ranas classify their concubines. A class A concubine has been in the household for a longer time than a class B. Their children are similarly classified."

On his mantelpiece is the face of Han Suyin, attractive, bright and as beautiful as any other sculptures of Nepalese women. We ask the ambassador how he got appointed to Nepal. "Any diplomat who is interested in art gets posted in Nepal, sooner or later. This is the perfect place for artists. There is clarity and harmony in the air and timelessness which comes with mountain living."

We jeep across to a nearby village to see a great lama, an *émigré* Buddhist priest from Tibet. We have an audience with him. He speaks twenty-four languages, and his first question to our guide is: What would we like on the language menu? After choosing English, we settle down in chairs made of tree bark to listen to the Buddhist priest. He talks like the editor of a posh magazine. He is suave, smooth, and grand. He lectures us about suffering and sacrifice, about having infinite love, about fleshly snares, about the necessity of meditation and pursuit after truth, about faith in the ancient wisdom. His

day consists of six hours of meditation, three hours
of prayers, four hours of instruction to his disciples.
He counsels us to follow his path. It is very strange,
because after Dom, in one of his gambits, has told
him about our "artistic pursuits" and said that we
were thinking of settling down in Nepal as permanent residents, he is no longer the great lama, the
ascetic Buddhist. He opens his cupboard and offers
us some homemade gin. "They don't have better gin
in England," he says. We drink it avidly, from imported glasses. His three wives serve us Chinese tea,
which has a kind of mixed flavor of jasmine and gin.
Then enormous plates of food are brought, after
which the great lama goes for a nap and we are en-
tertained by the many children of the household.
Disciples of all ages and both sexes drift in and out.
They seem to adore the great lama, for they come
bearing sweets and fresh vegetables — potatoes with
clinging mud, and tomatoes red and the size of
apples.

We walk to the center of the village in the afternoon. Prince can't go with us. He says he must get
back to Katmandu because there is a Communist
procession, the first such in Nepal to protest against
Dalda Ghee, a government-sponsored margarine
that, according to the Indian Communist Party, is
supposed to give people coronary thrombosis. There

is no evidence for this, but since the government now allows the sale of Dalda Ghee it is necessary that "people should know the truth."

All the adults are in the fields, except for a few old people draped over doorsills, sunning themselves. The village seems to be inhabited by children alone. They follow us in a procession of a hundred into the outskirts, on our way to the temple, and laugh at our feeble attempts to get through thickets and one-man trails. Dom says we must get horses tomorrow, because they would be more sure-footed. In Katmandu, we stop at the hotel of Han Suyin, which was once a very large palace. In the front hall we are surrounded with large glass cabinets containing Tibetan and Nepalese jewelry, ceramics, hand-printed cloth, carvings of horses and elephants and concubines, the famous concubines who have come down in history. The hotel has everything in it — expensive and cheap curios, rich and poor people, shell of a palace, atmosphere of a temple, display of an Oxford Street shop. It seems remote and recent and, as we pass through the hallways, some of them with walls like art galleries, I say to Dom, "It's like walking back in history. Strange that Nepal should be forty-five minutes away from India." At the bar we sit on stubs of trees and drink some imported whiskey, but we don't drink very much. We meet the ghost of Han Suyin. Look out of the window beyond and yonder towards the Tibetan border. The barman says he has come from India on foot, a week's journey. "How long did it take you to get here?" "Forty-five minutes. We came in a plane," I say. He looks down his nose.

In the evening there is a reception for Dom and me at the house of a poet. All the littérateurs of this tiny country meet us and treat us like celebrities. We are a bit embarrassed and uncomfortable, and pray that our Soho friends will not see an account of our reception in print. The beauty, the magic of Katmandu, the mystery of concubines and palatial halls, the delicate, natural people all make us want to be natural too, and it is difficult to be natural when being honored. Men twice our age sit with straight posture and read Nepalese poems in English and then wait for our judgment. But we have no offerings for the Nepalese gods. A terrible feeling because they do not ask for sacrifices of lambs but little tiny comments. We pity them and feel guilty and don't know what to say. Partly it is the reading; the tone is flat, and the words are lisped and whistled. Partly it is the translation, for English is very much a second language to the translators. Partly it is the nature of the poetry — Wordsworthian, just a little too mushy, a little too much of cows thinking pathetic fallacies.

We ask the rest of the poets to read their poems in Nepalese first, and somehow even the whistled words sound beautiful and are music to the ears — rhythm, intensity, power. And then the tedious English noise. Senses are confused. Perhaps some of them feel it, too, for a poet starts to read three poems and stops with one. It takes a little gentle persuasion before he reads on.

The man who is capable of judgment — a greater celebrity than we, the poet laureate of Nepal, L. P. Devkota, nicknamed Mount Everest — is not present. His absence is felt. Many people tell us about him: "He has done more for Nepal than any other man in history." "He is the greatest genius we can claim." "He is the jewel of our country." "He has made most of us famous." "He has no time for small talk." "No man thinks more than he does." "His conversation is oracular. It is never vacuous but always breathes emotion, passion, and wit."

We keep our eyes fixed on the door, thinking that the poet will walk in at any time with crown and scepter and make magic.

"When will he come?" I ask.

"Oh, didn't you know? He is dying. He's at Pashupatinath."

"What is that?" I ask.

"The greatest temple in the world."

There's a mysterious custom in Nepal. Men must die at the side of a river. The gods are kind, for four large rivers run through Nepal, so that there is no village from which a dying man cannot be carried to his unction by the water. Pashupatinath is on the bank of one river. "Devkota allows his relatives to carry him to the river, but laughs at the custom. Three times they have taken him, but he won't die, and so they return him to the hospital."

"How long did he stay?" Dom asks.

"Two, three days each time."

The picture is disturbing. Several dying men laid side by side on stretchers, waiting, as it were, in a queue to be received by the water. And the poets alone have the license to laugh.

After their recitation, the poets force me to make a formal presentation speech about Dom. I rise to the occasion; I mean, I realize there is no point in telling any private facts about Dom, for although they would suit the atmosphere of Soho or Chelsea, which Dom once likened to a warm animal, they are out of place in this fairyland of Katmandu, with its magical people and magical language. He was born, I announce, in 1938; wrote tiny poems from the age of five; wrote a book on cricket at twelve;

was admitted to Jesus College, Oxford, at eighteen; at nineteen wrote a tiny book that received a literary prize in England; and Dom is a legend. Dom thereupon says nice things about me and my writings, and, in his beautiful reading voice, he reads a poem of his called "A Letter to Dorothy." It is autobiographical — a sort of letter to love. Childhood in Bombay, where the sun rules the dung-smeared plains, chauffeurs drowse on hot verandas; exile, family trouble; rain in England, three winters of lust and playing drunken king, when poems grow like maggots in his head; and then the great good news — spring and love, the hawk and serpent touched. He reads it beautifully, more beautifully than anything he has read in India. In his Indian readings he was resentful, because he was not sure whether the people understood English poetry. "A Letter to Dorothy" is specially appropriate here — prosy, straightforward, images sensuous, common thought. It is effective because of the personal revelation it contains. It makes him the center of attention. The assembled talent regretfully plead the deficiencies of their language, the inability to translate their thoughts and feelings, manifold and towering, in Nepalese. "To be a poet in Nepalese is to die of frustration," one of them says. They wish they had been born in England. Our pity changes into sympathy, and the tenseness, the feeling of "I and thou," disappears. We are one. Dom reads a short poem about a Jesuit friend reading a river like a book of ancient wisdom, and then there is a libation, a praying for good fortune for one another, and we jeep across to the palace, silent and happy. The gods are good in Nepal. They live in Katmandu and ignore the people down south, who live in the shadow of the British raj, and with sunstroke, monsoons, and flood. Katmandu's sky is clear, all the stars are visible, and a good destiny is marked out.

Back at the palace, we have a tiny conversation with the servant given to us by the general. We are inquisitive and a bit tipsy from wine, stars, and delight. Dom asks him, "What do the seventy-eight maidens do?"

Embarrassment on the other side, but not so much as one expects. Understanding of our foreignness, I think. "They give pleasure in bed, and they bring silver pots for the Ranas," the servant says. The servant of enlightenment disappears in that natural, sweet way that we have come to regard as characteristically Nepalese.

We descend into our large beds, but the servant has chased away our sleep, and, what's more, he returns and says that if we had come before the revolution we would have been locked in with visitors sent as part of the hospitality. I regard this as another definition of revolution. Outside, the telephone wires sing duets with the crickets. We say good night to each other, and then I say a long prayer to the Nepalese gods. I compliment them on being so approachable, on giving men a chance to play, walk, and talk with them, on not living so far away, behind darkening clouds, as they do in the other countries. I compliment them also, without feeling inferior to them, on their pinkness, on having only pink clouds for their dress, on not winding sex in a sari, on a hundred other things, and by and by I float into a wonderful long sleep, and when I wake at noon, the soft sun lights the soft beauty of Katmandu.

It is two hours before the plane to Calcutta — back to the multitudes, back to the harsh sun, back to the dung-smeared earth. Our reporter guide, Prince, comes up to us. "You cannot go back to India until you've met Devkota," he says. We tremble. Neither one of us has been to a deathbed. We are terrified.

"No, thank you," I say. "We must go and pack."

"Don't tell me," Prince says chidingly, intimidatingly, "that you can't spare one half hour for a dying poet. He will be so flattered."

A poet laureate flattered by our visit?

Prince forces us into the jeep, and we are rattled toward the temple of death a few miles away.

What does one do? What does one say? We haven't spoken a word to each other. Prince is sitting in the front seat and we are in the back. And Dom says to me, or to himself, "You are being melodramatic." I have said nothing and I say nothing, but hold onto the steel frame of the jeep.

We are there at the river. From a distance it looks clear. It looks something like the Ganges, but the half-naked old women who are washing their clothes seem somehow prettier. There are the death chants, the mourning noises, the gnawing smell. We clamber up broken staircases, but our hearts are going down. We feel that the altitude is dropping somehow, and the heart is feeling the pull of gravity too much. We are in the room. It is the season of flies. I long to breathe spring air. I look around me — close to twenty relatives, the room crowded and hot. A woman is fanning a figure wrapped in white sheets. The figure hardly has face or features, but his shriveled hands feebly wave to us. Prince takes his position by the feet of the man. I don't know what to do. You see, the poet is lying on the floor, on a sort of mattress that covers the whole floor. There is no time to take off shoes. We have to sit quickly, relieve the tension of the room.

Through a window the stretchers of at least ten dying men are visible outside by the river. We can't keep our eyes on him, the poet. Soft groans. A very old man is breaking some ice and popping it into the poet's mouth. The woman goes on fanning. Prince introduces us in Nepalese. We can hear our names as Prince introduces us repeatedly. The poet gives us his hand. It's warm with life, and I feel calmed and soothed. He takes another piece of ice, and then the groans stop. He starts his speech slowly, as though he were drugged by death, but it is comforting to hear his voice. He thanks Prince for bringing these "two geniuses" from India. He seems to regard India as Dom and I regard England. He begins, "Christians are much better than we Hindus with death. They play music and they tell you about the heavenly angels sent for you, and the priest gives his unction with soft words and tells you if you really repent you will be taken up to Heaven. But Pashupati [the god of the animals] gives us Hindus no peace. He has robbed me of rest, he is cracking my soul. Pashupati will not give me any peace." Some more groans, then a smile of death plays on his face, ever so gently. "I don't know whether I believe in any of it. I would be better off in the hospital than here by the waters." A long pause. "I weighed two hundred pounds. Now I weigh ninety. You are seeing simply the skeleton of a man. Pashupati is cracking my soul and is burning me with cancer. No hell or fire could be worse than this. Give me your blessings, give your blessings to a dying man."

I stroke his hand and feel the Judgment Day.

He takes some more ice. "This is good," he says. "It quenches the fire. I wonder if there will be ice on the other side of the water. No torture could be worse than this cancer." His featureless face becomes more expressive, and I think perhaps he has said everything he has to say to all the relatives, and in this last moment of struggle he needs strangers.

Of Devkota's hundred written works only a few have been published. But he has tried to help the younger Nepalese poets. He asks what we think of his English translations and the anthology of Nepalese poetry that he edited, and is genuinely interested in our opinion. He says to Dom, "Will you recite some of your lines? I may not be able to understand now, but perhaps you could give me the gist of it."

First it is "A Letter to Dorothy," then poems about mountains and angels, then love and courage.

"I wish I had command over English like that," Devkota says. "Someone like you should learn Nepalese and translate us for the world. We have the feelings but not the language."

Then some words of gentle advice. He counsels us to make India great, to work, like Mr. Nehru, in spite of suffering and frustration. "Do your duty and do not look for recognition or rewards," he says. "This has been my creed, and it has helped me to live and make my contribution to Nepal."

Soft groans, softer and softer groans. There is a feeling of utter helplessness all around us, except for the woman fanning and the uncle cracking ice. "It is a matter of minutes now, and I shall be out on one of those stretchers and this will be the last time," he says. We grow aware of our clumsiness. I am grateful Dom can recite poems. Prince is looking out the window. Then he turns around and beckons to us to follow him. The poet is unconscious, so there are no words of parting to be said.

We go down the stairs awkwardly, feeling our way out of Pashupatinath. We jeep to the palace. Then there is a debate between Dom and me, the first words spoken since Pashupatinath, about what to give the servant. He is probably used to dinner jackets or gold chains, but we hand him our tiny rupee notes — as many as we can find in our coat

pockets. Out of the twists and turns of the halls;
a last, sweeping look over the chandeliers, the dimensionless; the servant brings the bags, and the
general comes down to bid us a brief good-by.

As our DC-3 takes off, the sky is threatening,
and we are not sure about the ability of the plane
to cut through the dense clouds. Soon the valley
shrinks to the size of a postage stamp. The nose of
the plane is directed toward Calcutta. Dom asks me
repeatedly whether the poems he recited to Devkota
were appropriate, and we end up talking about our
unhappiness at being taken for more than we were,
and about how our drinking friends in Soho would
never forgive us for blessing the dying poet. But
we console ourselves. The poet himself will forgive
us. It is time to sleep.

We wake in Calcutta. Darkness of the deep night
around us — steaming heat and torpor and Calcutta
feigning to be London. Stucco is English, but many-
colored stucco is Indian. The sun has bleached out
the color. Some taxis have two drivers, because it is
not safe for anyone, even a taxi driver, to go it
alone in Calcutta. We look for second-class hotels,
but we don't like their façades, and end up at the
Grand, which is the most expensive. Money-
changers everywhere; thousands of doorways to

staircases; a hotel for transients, people on the move.
The predatory bearers swarm, hungry for bak-
sheesh, even though the hotel is plastered with "No
Tipping" signs. In our rooms, we order drinks, and
two bearers carry them in, with an immense amount
of ice and a number of ice towels. Dom thumbs
through a telephone directory looking for people to
call; we can think of no one. I pick up the telephone
and put it down and have another drink. The heat
in Calcutta is like the heat of a brick wall. We drink
some more, and then we remember that prohibition
is not enforced in Calcutta, so we go out into the
streets. We hop into a taxi and say drive on. People
are dying on the streets, human corpses are strewn
like flies; women are giving birth to stillborn babies.
Dom says that we will have to learn to live with the
face of death in Calcutta. It is ten, and we are still
driving around on a sightseeing tour of Calcutta
with our eyes shut. Then we finally gain courage
and ask one of the drivers to recommend a "bar
with life," and he drives us through slums and slums
— little dark doorways and unpainted wooden
gates. He tells us a grisly story about people being
knifed in bars, and wouldn't we like to go back to
the Grand? Some of the bars we pass are closed, and
the driver says it is too late for a bar with life. But
we persist, and have him wait outside a dingy en-

trance. The bar has nothing in common with English ones. No nucleus of sober people — just drunk after drunk, or tables with solitary girls of every possible nationality and color. We pass between tables lined up by the hundred, and look for a bar with a rail and stools. The rooms are dark and the music is loud, and the waitress thinks we are looking for trouble and pops us down at a table and insists on three drinks each and says we won't be alone too long.

We leave the drinks and money on the table and retreat into our taxi. I want to go to a bar with a rail and stools. The driver thinks we are looking for trouble, and says he has a family of seven waiting for him and all the nice girls are gone from the streets and bars and there is no point in wandering. We have nowhere to go, so he shifts us into another taxi, with a driver who drives fast and recklessly. This one says lots of bars are open, and takes us to a zoo, where monkeys, gorillas, and gibbons are being served drinks, and lots of sheep, pretending to be women, are crying in the corners, but we have found the bar with the rail and stools. We are served imported brandy, but it tastes like methylated spirits. We drink a quantity of it. Dom asks me whether I would like to go to Shillong, in Assam, and spend some weeks there studying the Nagas,

the last of the head-hunters — or would I rather go
to Sikkim, which is like Nepal? We think of many,
many ways of getting out of Calcutta. But we take
to the methylated spirits as ducks to water, and before long we are looking around the bar for little
Siamese girls or tiny Persian women who would just
talk to us about our troubles and depression. The
barman asks us if we would like to meet some
people. "First-class Ango-Indian girls," he says. "Or
European. But if you don't mind some dirty color,
I have some beautiful children who will give you
a good time." We go out into the street, and back
to our taxi.

A series of disastrous accidents. First, as we taxi
through one of those darkened streets, a blowout,
and we lose our trustworthy taxi driver. From the
street, we enter a small, square room where there is
an ugly dancer, riddled with all the diseases under
the sun, who dances to all the scratchy records and
changes the needle more than she shuffles her feet.
She pleads an empty stomach. A quilted floor, with
round pillows for back rests. The harmonium
players and the breathless tabla players and the girl
of sixteen who dances and pulls at her hair and
makes lascivious gestures and sings, "Nightingale is
knocking at your door. Why don't you say come
in?" She sings until one can almost see her lungs

hanging out between her lips. We want to go home. Pimps are alerted from door to door, and there is no way out of the streets. A new, less dependable pair of taxi drivers are cleaning out our pockets. They insistently and slowly take us from door to door, and rows of girls come up to the side of the car, and we take refuge by saying, "No, no." The girls walk away insulted and angry. Some of them say, "You are inhuman and callous." We give them some money. We spot another taxi standing, and, after paying our drivers, jump out of our car into it. "The Grand — quickly, the Grand!" One of the drivers starts the car — a long, rumbling sound in the engine, then an even hum. We sigh with relief. Before the taxi moves an inch, a man jumps halfway through the front window beside the unoccupied taxi driver. He straddles the door — an ugly, bony face peering at us with bloodshot eyes, a hand holding a ridiculous little penknife. The unoccupied taxi driver and the man on the window fight. The other driver accelerates the car and rushes through the street like a madman. The front door, which the man is straddling, opens and sags with the burden, but he clings on. He wraps his hands around the back door, and both Dom and I get down on the floor. Then there is the most terrifying scream, which rings through the streets like a death gong.

Indian Summer

The taxi driver has the figure by his testicles, and before Dom and I can get any words out of our throats the figure is dropped on the street and left. "Stop! Stop!" we shout at the driver. "You've murdered him." But the car is still rushing through the streets. The driver is trying to close the front door. He bangs the door violently and repeatedly. "The bloody man was a robber. He got what he deserved." Then we see the large, blinking neon sign: THE GRAND. A driver gives us one big push out of the taxi. Before we recover, the car disappears into the alley and the dark night.

Upstairs, we collapse in our chairs. Our wallets have been pinched by the taxi driver. We watch the dawn creep in through the window, and I feel heavy, as though I were carrying some dead weight.

Dom and I don't see each other the next morning until noon; we just stay in bed. And then Dom comes over and we sit at the table and ring for the bearer. Dom says he doesn't want anything to drink; coffee will do. The bearer doesn't understand about our new interest in coffee. We drink coffee until two-thirty, and Dom paces nervously, sometimes stopping at the window. But there's nothing to see. It looks out on the courtyard and on other windows. Some of them still have their shades down.

Dom starts reciting poetry. He has an excellent memory — a sort of poet's memory. He's not good at analyzing things or explaining them, but he's excellent at remembering poems and conversations. By three-thirty, we are our usual selves, because we have cheered each other with odd poems.

I wonder if there are any people like Narayana or Khushwant here, and both of us simultaneously start thumbing through the telephone directories. Bengal is the house of literature, and this time a thousand names come to mind. We ring up the poet Sudhindra Datta, but he's in America. The painter Jamini Roy doesn't have a telephone. We put down the telephone, and Dom drinks his twentieth glass of water. We slump on the comfortable divans and reminisce about our host in Nepal. Somehow we run through our stock of amusing stories quickly, and we both begin to pace nervously.

Dom rings for the bearer, and I notice that he has gone off water. After a couple of drinks, I switch to tomato juice. We call the poet Buddhadeva Bose on the telephone, and reach him. We stop feeling friendless. Bose would love to come for drinks, and he wishes to bring his cousin and an American poet. At seven o'clock, we try to find our way downstairs but get lost in the halls. We pass though an enormous room — hundreds and hundreds of people. A very loud, smoky cabaret. Someone is singing through a hundred loudspeakers, and the loudspeakers seem to be vying with one another. We rush through the maze, feeling tired and unhappy, and down flights and flights of steps. We go into the Scheherazade Bar and wait and wonder about Bose's appearance. I long for a breath of fresh air, but Dom says he can't face the people outside. "Besides, there's no fresh air there," he says. "We are in a desert."

Bose arrives with his cousin and the American poet. Bose is a little man, Napoleonic, with a nervous face, animated eyes. He doesn't look like a poet, but he recognizes Dom as one. We go out on the veranda, because Bose is suffocated in the bar. We drink to each other's good health and then take a large taxi to Bose's house. People cling to the car, thrusting their emaciated hands in the windows. The cousin puts up the windows. The American poet doesn't say very much. Gentle, handsome face, bangs of hair turning gray. The cousin says there are ten people in India who know how to write English; he and his cousin are two of the ten.

Bose is terribly nice, and upstairs in his little house he shows us his writings — scores of books in Bengali. He is the modern Tagore, but he lacks a translator. The American poet says that if he can find money he will spend a year in Bengal learning Bengali and then translate Bose for the world. The cousin says, "I have had precisely the same thing in mind, but then, on second thought, I think I ought to get on with my own creative work." The cousin reminds us about the big bills at the Grand and suggests we should come and live with him and talk art. We have dinner — fish with bones, which we enjoy separating. And after the fish we have liqueurs and talk of Tagore and Bengali literature, culture, and communism.

But somehow Calcutta doesn't seem to be Delhi. It lacks the magic of our meetings with Khushwant, Narayana, Mr. Chatterji. And the strange thing is I am sure I like Bose just as much as the others. But things have changed. During the conversation, I have long lapses when I stop thinking, when I am there but not really there. My Oxford cigarette is burning very low, and if I am not careful the fag end will scorch my lips. There don't seem to be very many draws left.

When we leave, Bose comes along, and we visit Jamini Roy. "Jamini Roy," Bose tells us, "is one of the great artists of India, but his reputation has suffered in the last few years and the reason is a strange one. He is so generous to his pupils and disciples that he signs their copies of his paintings."

Each of his paintings, therefore, has many originals. This has led to confusion — bizarre auctions when everyone bids for what they think is the original.

I think I've never met a man like Jamini Roy — kind and compassionate, a grandfather to the human race. But somehow I can't make any effort to reach him, and continually find myself looking away toward a blank spot on the wall. Bose says he will arrange a party for us and gather some men of letters. But I cannot bring myself to be excited.

We are back in the Grand. Dom says that after Bose's party he will leave Calcutta and go to Sikkim, then to Bombay and back to England. He asks me whether I'd like to come to Sikkim too. "It will be like Nepal," he says. "A pocket of private and delicious happiness." But I must go to Delhi. "I don't think I'll stay on for the party," I say. "I need a complete change. I think I will leave tomorrow."

Next day, I say good-by to Dom. Dom insists that he must come to the airport, because he doesn't know when we will see each other again. Another leave-taking, and then a Viscount. I pinch myself, as I often do when I am going through a mad waking dream; then I look nervously at my hands for the impressions of my nails, and I am relieved to find them there. The Viscount, once it is off the ground and the whistling sound has stopped, sounds like thunder — monsoon thunder, which makes protracted gurgling sounds before a blast — and I don't feel very well. I feel as if I were speeding away — far, far away from Oxford. It seems that my pilgrimage up north is over. The collecting of exhibits is over. The bummy period has ended. I feel old.

V | WINTER OF CONTENT

DELHI begins to cool. It is too early for the mountain winds, and as always winter is slow in coming. But we stop sleeping on the veranda, stop being wakened by crows at dawn. The mosquito nets are put away because winter is coming, and the doors and windows shut against what flies and mosquitos remain. The summer of discontent is ending.

In Delhi it never gets very cold. Although at night everyone must sleep with blankets, in the daytime the edge of the winter is broken by the soft sun.

At home Mother engages a tailor, who comes about nine-thirty in the morning and stays for seven or eight hours to make winter clothes for the family. He does his own measuring, cutting, and sewing, and is as good with English suits as he is with shirts and casual wear.

The tailor sits on our veranda. He has been working for us for many years. In the days before we fled from Pakistan, he made my rompers and knee pants, and when I graduated to wearing long pants he put them on me and slapped my behind three or four times to remind me of my manhood. "But," he added quickly, "Ved Sahib, you will always be a boy to me."

Our tailor is Indian in his ways. He is not methodical. He is slow, spontaneously jocular, and can entertain us for weeks with the saga of his family. He seems to remember every little thing that happened to his grandparents, aunts and uncles, nieces and nephews. He will tell the sahib all the family troubles — how he is forced to work so many hours, and how difficult it is to pay for his children's education, and would it be possible to get his son a job in a government office, and couldn't you speak to so and so about his daughter, who would like to serve in a good house and who would be a very faithful servant? When he has the ear of a sahib he grumbles, and for a piece of good work he expects to be rewarded with favors. We feel personally involved with him.

Unlike many other Indian tailors, our tailor is never on the lookout for new clients. All his customers seem to be of twenty years' standing. He always complains about the many demands made of him. Recently he was persuaded by a patron of nearly half a century to take on a new job. This, the last exasperating demand, he was unable to refuse. After all, Prasad Sahib, the President of India, is in need. "At first I didn't possibly think I could take on his work too. It is not just a matter of doing a job for Prasad Sahib. He has dozens of children and grandchildren. Well, if I take on his house I have to take on a whole new world of customers, and I'm old and overworked."

Our tailor, though modest in appearance, claims he can change a man by changing the style of his clothes. He can transform babu into sahib, sahib into officer. Saint, beggar, bapu (father) — nothing is beyond him. His confidence is unnerving, and the only thing that makes him real is his endless family saga.

He is very anxious to make me a new suit using my English clothes as models. He longs to rival English tailors, but many of his customers are politicians and have stopped wearing English clothes.

"Sahib, may I make you a suit?"

I seldom go out now and one light woolen suit is enough.

"No thank you. I don't need a new suit," I reply. Instead I ask him to make me another pair of pajamas and kurta (a long collarless shirt which hangs around the body like a sack). Loose pajamas and kurta are now my comfortable, homely dress. The tailor is disappointed because this simple Indian dress demands no craftsmanship, no special tailoring.

I stay at home more and more now and hardly ever change into a suit, though whenever I go out I wear my English suit because I have grown used to it and it still seems dignified. Even my tailor can't redo a man overnight. But I am no longer aware of hand-sewn collars, three front buttons, and two slits in the back of the coat. I couldn't care less about gentlemanly elegance.

The tailor is the last of our old servants, the two house servants are new. I feel a bond with him because he has watched me through my changing years.

I can hear the slap of my bare feet when as a child I raced with forbidden street children, the old servants watching and scolding and flattering, the tailor among them shouting, "Watch out for your clothes," and in the same breath, "Don't stop, get on with you." They smiled whether I won or lost. This was loyalty. Sometimes my parents reproved me for being too close to the servants, but when they were out in offices and shops, parties and clubs, the servants remained home as companions and storytellers. The children next door moved away, their father transferred to another district. But the servants grew up with us. They never changed.

The tailor sits on the veranda of our new house, turning the wheel of his machine. I recline on the small lawn in front of the veranda and look at him from my wicker chair. I am thirsty. I get up and bring two glasses of water, one for the tailor and one for myself. "Sahib, you should have asked me to get you some water. Don't you like me any more?" "What is the difference?" I ask. I sit back in my chair and look at him. He is lean and frail with a chest clamped between round shoulders, a bald head and a yellowed beard rich with color of age. He stops turning the wheel, leaves his stool on the veranda, and comes and sits on the ground at my feet. "Take this chair, take this chair," I say, nervously standing up. He puts both his gaunt hands on my knees and I drop back into the chair. "Sahib, don't you like me any more? It's little things about you that trouble me. You won't let me cut you a suit like your English one because you don't trust me. You don't let me get you a glass of water because you don't like me. What has England done to you?" He won't remove his hands from my knees and he stubbornly keeps his position on the ground. "Look here, tailor, I don't want an English suit because I am comfortable in pajamas and kurta." "Sahib, I don't understand the world. Why have people stopped wearing suits? Why have all the Indian gentlemen started wearing ugly black coats with buttoned-up collars? Why does everyone want to look like their poor tailor? What is going to happen to my profession? When I saw you in the beautiful English suit, my heart went out to you. The deputy high commissioner who used to live next door to you in the old days — do you remember him? He had a suit just like yours. Won't you let me cut you another? Never mind the rest of my customers. I'll work for you, Sahib, day and night, and it will be the best suit made in Delhi this year." "But, tailor," I say, "you don't understand. A new English suit is the last thing I need. And about the water — I can get it as well as you can." "Ved Sahib, your old servant and friend though I am, I would rather have you kick me than bring me a glass of water."

I try to explain to the tailor that he and I should be able to get each other water without his being hurt. But he sits at my feet holding my knees and refuses to accept my explanation. He feels offended. I stand up and nervously motion him to sit down in the chair. He looks even more hurt and shakes his puzzled beard. "What has England done to you? I don't understand. I could never sit in that chair and you know it. I have never sat in a chair and I don't want to."

As in the old days, the understanding really comes from him. I sit down. "Maybe I'm just old," he says. "Maybe I'm just ancient. Many of these young servants would like nothing better than a soft chair; they would let this grass grow under their feet until they were buried in it. They wouldn't lift a hand to cut it. By their rebellion they dig their own graves, and Sahib, you aren't helping them learn their station by offering them chairs." "Tailor, there is no station. Everyone must make his own station." "No, Sahib. We are born into our station." He points to his scarred forehead. "My station is written here." Then he points to my forehead. "Your station is written there. It is all in the books of Karma and Dharma. My Karma says I must be a tailor and my Dharma says I must do my duty by my sahibs." "Tailor, these are old ideas." "I am an old man," he says, and he runs a finger through his yellowed beard. "But, Sahib, I am wise. You can no more change my station than I can change yours. You will marry in your caste and I will marry my son to a girl in our own caste. You will send your children to England to be educated and I will teach my grandsons to be good tailors."

No, there never can be intermarriages between castes because his son will never have the education to marry above his station. No one can ever be swept away by love when marriages are arranged. Marriages must be arranged because the parents' security and comfort in old age depend completely on their children.

The older and the younger generations must be kept together. And so life must be perpetuated, so it must go on. No one can change the system because the system is life. The tailor acknowledges that perhaps the times are changing. Some day all will be educated, but not yet.

Though he loves Englishmen and therefore England, he chides me for my English ways. "Sahib," he says, "you're Indian and not English." Then he returns to his machine and spins the wheel circle upon circle, stopping now and again to give me counsel. He recommends a visit to Haridwar, where for untold centuries, Indians have washed away their sins and deposited the ashes of their dead. At Haridwar is the source of the Ganges, in folklore, the first spring of water in the Indian plains. It was the first water from the mountain, the great gift of God.

The suggestion strikes me as bizarre. My English self recoils from the centuries of superstition behind his words. But somehow I feel impelled to go to Haridwar.

A few days later I go to Haridwar. The tailor has admonished me not to wear my new pajamas and kurta until I am washed in the Ganges, and though I take his admonition lightly, I have brought them with me in a small case. Just to please the fancy of an old man — that is what I say to myself.

I want to travel in a third-class compartment with India, as Gandhi did, but my family cautions against it, there is danger of disease.

This is my first train ride in India since my return. I like my carriage well enough, with open windows, the seat covered with soot, the ineffective fan buzzing, and the blackening wind rushing in until it is impossible to make any conversation. I don't care about the people in my first-class compartment because they are in English dress with money in their pockets.

In the train my eyes open to country scenes: Gandhi's India — peasants with loincloths around their bodies, working on the land tending the animals. Shifting images pass before my eyes. Victorian, civil service, English India with tremulous whispers about sex and smoking-room banter. Polit-

ical India with circus legislatures. Intellectual India
with a Sanskrit text. Indias are endless.

People come to Haridwar with jars containing
the ashes of their dead. They come to wash their
sins, to be reinvigorated, to be cured of faults and
diseases. The station at Haridwar is their hotel. Men,
women, children eat and sleep there. The cows mill
through streets as if they owned them. Drivers hoot
impatiently. Religious music played by beggar saints
drones continuously. At the river I take my shoes off
and walk along the bank until I find an uncrowded
place. The Ganges, like the slow-moving Isis at Oxford, smells rank. A woman at my left drops some
ashes in the river while reciting a Sanskrit prayer.
I hold my breath, take a quick dip in the river, and
rub myself vigorously with a towel. Then I put on
my tailor's clothes. Around me men and women
stand half naked and say their prayers. Nepal doesn't
seem very far away; the pilgrims at Haridwar look
like the Nepalese.

The genealogists — the Pandas — of India's hundreds of districts dwell at Haridwar. I walk up and
down the bank looking for the Panda of my village
— my Panda, the Panda of Bhaini, Punjab. I find
my Panda in an ancient tenement, sitting on his
wooden bed, surrounded by folio volumes written

in large letters and coarse hands. When I tell him my village and name he opens the proper volume to my genealogy and then begins reading the history of my family. Mehta, Ved Parkash, son of Amolak Ram, son of Bhola Ram, son of Gian Chand, son of Karm Chand, son of Ram Jas Mal, son of Pardhana Mal, son of Mansa Ram, son of Budhwant Rai. Amolak Ram, from his wife, Shanti Devi, daughter of Durga Das, begot seven children: Promila Kumari, Nirmal Kumari, Urmil Kumari, Om Parkash, Ved Parkash, Usha Kumari, Ashok Kumar. Bhola Ram, from his wife. . . . The Panda runs over our birth dates, names, generations. For half an hour he recites name after name after name. I stop him when he reads of my grandfather Bhola Ram's coming to Haridwar with the ashes of his father. "That's nonsense," I say. "He lived more than two hundred miles from here and he would have had to travel for days on foot and horseback, in bullock carts, tamtams and trains. He could not have left the village for that long." But then I look at the Panda's book, and the hand is unmistakably my grandfather's. The Panda explains, "Remember what he was doing, depositing the ashes of his father in the blessed Ganges. No hazard was too much, no journey was too long."

I copy down the genealogies for my mother. The

Walking the Indian Streets

Panda records my pilgrimage in his book. I give him a thank offering, and as I leave he says, "Now you must lead a new life."

I'm off with his injunction to clean my slate. I wear my new suit of clothes, and with no family to caution me, return home in a third-class compartment — part of Gandhi's India.

All through my journeys among the politicians and bureaus and through the villages where mud huts and hovels pass for homes, a bit of an acre for a farm, a hand plow for a tractor, a money lender and a blacksmith for progress, naked unhealthy bodies for human beings, ruins of a temple for the spiritual life, a handful of rice or corn for a meal from the beneficent God, one memory shines — Sunday lunch with Prime Minister Nehru.

At lunch the Prime Minister eats with his hands, but gives his guest a fork. I sit on his right, and his daughter, Mrs. Gandhi, is to my right, and his two quiet grandsons in their teens make up the rest of the party. Mrs. Gandhi calls the Prime Minister "Papu" — which seems to be a mixture of Papa and "Bapu." All of a sudden I feel that Gandhiji, the Bapu (Father) of India, is there and the light hasn't gone out.

With his Gandhi cap on, the Prime Minister does

not look old, but when he takes it off he looks his age. He has spent the morning in the hospital getting himself thoroughly checked by the doctors and they say he will live for at least fifteen or twenty years more. He admits he has led a very strenuous life — long separation from family and friends, nine years in British prisons, unbroken periods of lonely counsel. He was left alone to guide India in its glory by the unseasonable death of the Bapu, Mahatma Gandhi. His aristocratic birth, his agnosticism, his faith in science and industrial society stood between Gandhi and him, but the man who shot the Mahatma for trying to quell the Hindu fury against the Muslims misunderstood the bond between Jawaharlal, the disciple, and Gandhi, the guru. A bullet could not touch Gandhi's spirit. At his death the entire nation mourned for weeks. I remember weeping as I listened to Nehru's tragic speech, "The light has gone out of our lives." Once Bapu's triumphant spirit seemed no more, India's future was precarious and the Prime Minister modestly acknowledges his contribution to her survival. Had he not withstood the shock of Gandhi's death, India might have been robbed forever of the light of independence.

Even before the bearer finishes crowding the brass plate with half a dozen little cups containing rice, vegetables, curry and condiments, I'm struck by something that has been present throughout my visit with the Prime Minister but that I have just now recognized. His features are pure Brahmin; his buttoned-up coat and tight pajamas seem Mughal; his presence is nobly Indian. When he speaks Hindi it radiates ancient beauty; when he speaks English he has the regal air of a king in durbar. Speaking to an Oxford graduate of twenty-five, he shows a youthful companionship which takes me by surprise. His intellectual grasp appears Indian and Western, ancient and modern. I recognize him. I feel I am confronting Sanskrit, Mughal, and English India at one time; he expresses the three Indias with their extremes but without their contradictions. His face suggests harmony, clarity, quintessence of beauty.

Mrs. Gandhi is the official hostess for the Prime Minister. She is also President of the Congress Party and is the first woman of India. But her pre-eminence is hidden beneath the delicate charm with which she graces the luncheon. She prefers to listen to the Prime Minister than to talk herself.

As a child, I was forced to eat yoghurt, and grew to regard it as an important issue dividing families and men, but having failed to eat rice and curry with my hands, I quickly gulp the yoghurt Mrs. Gandhi serves me and apologize to the Prime Minister for turning a family lunch into a serious question period. He smiles. There are long silences between questions and answers, and these silences, in any other circumstances nerve-racking, in his presence become restful.

While talking, we touch on the unfortunate division of India among religions, races, castes and language groups, and the Prime Minister points to the troubled history that entangles modern India. Despite the divisions India manages to survive and go forward. In part its progress is a compliment to the history of British administration, British law and order, but the compliment is soured by the conscious or unconscious policy of division which sometimes accompanied their administration. Besides, law and order are conventions which often gloss over rather than honestly face differences. Again I feel the real secret of one free India lies in the Prime Minister. His character reconciles and resolves the various Indias. The real battle will come after his death, when the many fighters will knock each other down, leaving the horses to dart willy-nilly.

When Nehru is tired he lies down and puts himself to sleep by reading. Last night he was reading a recent lecture by C. P. Snow delivered in Cambridge. Having been at one time a scientist, he feels with Snow the dangers of increasing specialization which is one of the more serious consequences of modern society. He is never too busy to read and tries to keep up with contemporary thought. His reading includes everything from poetry to zoology. He is not sure how many leaders have time to read, but he modestly maintains there must be quite a few. After lunch we return to the sitting room. Mrs. Gandhi has the air-conditioner turned off because "Papu" finds the room too cool. "The air-conditioner," she says, "is more for the benefit of the guests than for Papu." He has learned to live with the heat. I think I should leave, but the Prime Minister is relaxed and would love to talk.

He reminisces about his Cambridge days. He doesn't know why he hasn't written much about Cambridge in his autobiographies. He was a solitary boy in England. But, he adds, "Those ancient universities are really good. They leave a lasting influence." It is a mistake when Oxford and Cambridge men try to recreate their universities in India. We cannot ever go back to the universities exactly as we left them. On returning to the universities, many of the graduates are disappointed. Fun at the university is like adolescence, and adolescence cannot be recovered, at least not by those who feel a social calling. And there is so much need for social feeling and responsibility. India is a good example of what remains to be done in the world. The developed societies seemed to have reached their peaks and sometimes they feel uncertain and frustrated with their wealth. But in India the frustration is of a different sort. It comes of too much instead of too little to do.

The Prime Minister admits the Indians have not always responded to their calling. In Sanskrit, for example, the literature to be discovered, annotated and analyzed is endless. Yet the Germans were the first to deal with our literature in a scientific and scholarly way. They gave us a lead in this which was followed subsequently by Indian scholars.

Sitting beside him and being talked to, as hundreds of promising and unpromising young people must have been talked to by Gandhi, I can fathom the bond, the relationship which must exist between a disciple and a guru.

The simple sophistication of the Prime Minister leads me to wonder about the great Oxford figures who delighted in pretensions and eccentricities. They represented a nonconformist spirit continually trying to break through prescribed modes. The spirit was always searching to distinguish itself from the drab, the usual, the banal. And when sometimes the nonconformists, in their enthusiasm, exceeded the bounds, the academic community forgave the excesses because it commended the nonconformist spirit. As a result of my English education I was prepared to meet some condescension from a great man and, in an unrestrained moment, I tell the Prime Minister how surprised I am at being able to speak to him so naturally.

This turns our conversation to England. The Prime Minister thinks England is still the most conservative country in all Europe and, despite the great social revolution since World War II, is still quite class conscious. History spared England a sweeping revolution and this tended to entrench her in her preserved prejudices, and coming as we do from our caste-ridden society, we are in a good position to appreciate both the advantages and the disadvantages of conservative society.

With a youthful smile he admits that if an Indian is blessed with graces and educated in the ways of English society he can be very happy in England. Indeed he is quite aware that some Indians, even today, prefer the certainties of the dead English raj to the uncertainties of freedom. He agrees that the choice between authority and freedom is not just Indian but is as old as history. It is in another form the choice between being a contented animal or Socrates. But, he adds with compassion, we must not judge harshly. "We are children of habit and habit is not easily changed." He agrees that we are torn in

our loyalties to British and our own India, one with
established standards, the other at present lacking in
standards. In British India we race with a handicap
because all that we can do is often done better by an
Englishman. Indian India is naturally our own, but
it will take a long time before we can reach a Western degree of advancement. Meanwhile we are condemned to fall between the two worlds and tolerate
an existence more superficial than satisfactory.

He questions me about my education, interests,
and what I should like to do in life. He recommends
a career of writing and admits India's need for more
writers, painters, sculptors, musicians and dancers.
But, he adds candidly, "While India needs people
like you, I'm not sure she can at present really afford them." India, he explains, has so many funda-
mental needs to resolve that he doesn't know when
we will get beyond them and be able to subsidize
culture, as we would like to, in a major way. He
feels, however, that difficulties can be stimulating,
and points to many of our creative and scholarly
works that have been done with world acclaim but
under impossible conditions. In time he recommends
a return home for me. He says it will not be easy,
but worthwhile men never shrink from hazards and
hardships. I feel cheered as never before. I feel the
problems we are facing are of epic proportions and

men of duty must measure up to the heroic possibilities. While heroism seems to be playing out in the West, it is just beginning in the East.

Mr. Nehru, for one, doesn't seem to be sitting on the issues. He walks and talks, and moves from subject to subject with ease. It seems his India is in its gestation period and may be longer at it than our cherished elephants.

The Prime Minister prays for peace. He hopes the new India will be given a chance to show her mettle. He prays that we will not be stunted in our growth. He hopes for better times than we have known in our century. In this, he adds, he is no different from anyone else. But when many are paralyzed with depression, it is left to the thinking and pioneering men to break fresh ground.

He says his work is not always intellectually engaging and thanks me for talking with him. I am left aghast and wonder how the Prime Minister of India can spare time for private individuals. His parting words to me are, "Come and talk to me whenever the spirit moves you." "I wouldn't know the protocol." "Just ring up my secretary. It is as easy as that." I come away feeling that Nehru is as great as Gandhi and that circumstances have prevented him from shaping younger leaders. It is easy for Prasads to yield their lives for a movement, but it is much more difficult for young Prasads to commit themselves to the thankless day-by-day routine of building a nation with bricks and mortar.

I remember Dom remarking after an interview with the Prime Minister that he was doing with India what poets do with words. When the press reported this remark, a common friend asked me if everyone must become a sycophant of the Prime Minister.

After the lunch the answer is clear to me. There is a difference between a sycophant and a disciple — one is empty and spineless, the other has opinions, even at the time of instruction.

Gandhi's followers were wracked with family dissensions and quarrels. Indeed, two of Gandhi's most powerful disciples, Jawaharlal Nehru and Vallabhai Patel, were very different from him and from each other in their attitudes and approaches. Although Gandhi never stopped open criticism and full discussion, he commanded to the last the unswerving loyalty and obedience of all his followers, despite the fact that he was a referee of his movement who also made the rules.

I come away from the Prime Minister feeling that my Indian experience has acquired yet another depth. My bummy holiday is finished forever. Indian summer has changed into another and better season and there is promise. The problems aren't so huge that they need stop movement of the limbs. I'm finding elbow room in the crowd. I'm learning to walk the Indian streets.

Once more I am in a plane. I am returning to the West, the indulgent West, but this time my journey has direction. I am not shunting from plane to plane, from taxi to taxi, as in the bummy days. I must complete my Western education before I settle in India.

I open my journal and begin thumbing through my impressions of the summer in India. Keeping a journal may seem a Victorian habit, but my journal is not an anachronism. It is lifelike — humdrum, disjointed, untidy, and without an index. It does not even have dates. I refuse to date my entries because I loathe chronology. For me, experience is amorphous, and until I look away from it, or see it from a distance, I can never shape it into a rounded whole, can never give it form. I lean on my journal as a record of revealing moments — the photographs of happenings as I focused on them at the time.

I take my eyes off the journal and look out the window. There is not much to see. The Indian land mass is obscured beneath leaden clouds. The clouds are dense but they are not the frightening thunderheads of the monsoons. The jet rides like a large bus wheeling its way through snow, but without skids and jerks. This Comet is not at all like the DC-3 that took me to Nepal and the Viscount that carried me away from Calcutta — its motor has the even hum of a smooth and powerful machine, and after a while, like a factory worker, I become accustomed to the noise.

I nod to the hostess, who is quite charming. She talks of inconsequentials — the weather, the distance to Karachi.

I return to the journal.

Page 200. Today, received letter from great friend at Balliol, Jasper Griffin. Takes exception to my letter about days with Dom: "What is this awful word bummy with which you make so free? I never heard it from you — or indeed from anyone — in Oxford. Nor were you really as dissolute and irresponsible as you try to make out; though you won't thank me for reminding you of the fact, you were actually a pillar of respectability and straight living — even to your daily dark suit; you were even abstemious with drink. You are an old fraud, and I have a mind to denounce you to the public as the moral man you are." Doesn't understand — writers, like cats, must live several lives. Life is bundle of little truths; art is a way to greater truth.

Walking the Indian Streets

I look for my last meeting with the Prime Minister, the Mahatma of lunch.

Page 202. Today I saw him again, really a man of many faces, all beautiful. Not only Brahmin, regal, English, but ingenious politician, saint, good theoretician. Face so expressive, more photogenic than any I have seen. Face to win confidence anywhere.

Page 204. "If you feel you must go, you must. Your project is worthwhile. You are right to follow your interests and go in search of your documents. You will not turn your back on the problems and the country. There are all kinds of activity. If I had not been drawn into politics, I would have taken up writing. Not fiction — I lack that sort of imagination." (Dom: Doing with India what poets do with words.)

Page 205. Very understanding, mysterious ability to fix people in a fraction of a moment and see the whole. Quality of an artist to see in a moment something permanent and eternal.

The hostess comes up and serves me some coffee. "The weather," she says, "is not bad. We will be soon clear of it." The land is still veiled in clouds. They have thinned out a bit and I can make out the jungles through the haze.

It is difficult to find anything in my journal and the jungle of impressions and disconnected experiences makes bad reading. The summer in India is blurred and misty. My most lucid entries are bracketed comments, asides sprinkled at random.

Page 1. [Without words, man would be locked in a telephone booth shouting to the world over a disconnected phone. Wires are words, the telephone directory is a dictionary.]

Page 27. [Government campaign to rid Hindi of English words wrong. Waste of energy making Sanskrit concoctions for telephones, airplanes, engines. Pure language or pure race nonexistent. Language grows through use, experience, corruption, and our vocabulary must include Sanskrit and English experience.]

Page 53. [Wonder if there can be great Indian novel in English. Could Tolstoy have expressed Russia without writing in Russian? In vernaculars, novel writing is just discovered. There is hardly any tradition of the novel, no feeling for past experiments and mistakes. They seem as new to the art as Daniel Defoe.]

Page 60. [Just read 53. Conrad — a great writer using a foreign language.]

Page 63. [Many problems come down to one of finding standards. For a century we lived under English standards but they did not give us many opportunities to equal them. We produced carbon copies of their literature and newspapers, administration, officers. Can we make our own standards? How long will it take?]

Walking the Indian Streets

On page 107, I decided asides were intrusions clogging the narrative and dropped them. I have no patience with authors who punctuate their stories with running commentaries on their private emotions. The story must be made to speak for itself.

We are flying over the Indian Ocean and there isn't a single cloud in sight; it is beautifully clear. I have slept on my impressions and asides and feel refreshed. The hostess brings me some paper and I begin to make notes on my journal, rearranging facts and days, trying to give some order and shape. First I go through the journal copying out the names of all the people I saw, I talked to: the Pakistani friend, the music master, Charlton, the President, Jai Parkash Narayan, Khushwant Singh, Narayana Menon, L. P. Devkota.

I string the names like prayer beads. Touching them, I call up many experiences.

Lightning Source UK Ltd.
Milton Keynes UK
UKHW020731131119
353452UK00007B/742/P